Ariane d'Hoop
The Slightest Attachment

MatteRealities / VerKörperungen: Perspectives from Empirical Science Studies | Volume 27

Editorial

Since the late 1970s, empirical science studies have developed into a key field of research at the intersection of science, technology and society. This field merges a repertoire of theories and methods stemming primarily from cultural anthropology, sociology, linguistics and history. Its main characteristic is the detailed analysis of scientific practices and epistemic cultures and how these become entangled with public discourses and everyday life. This focus tries to reveal specific, local configurations and their epistemological as well as social consequences. Beyond a mere deconstruction, science studies are constantly looking to engage with the fields in which they do their work. The goal of this book series is to offer to scholars a German and English speaking Forum that

- develops inter- and trans-disciplinary bodies of knowledge in the areas of medicine and the life sciences and makes these nationally and internationally available;
- supports young scientists through opening up a new field of work which runs across existing disciplinary structures;
- encourages the formation of tandems through co-authorship. In particular, it supports, evaluates and comments on collaborative projects with colleagues from the natural and engineering sciences.

The series is directed towards scholars and students from both the empirical science/social studies and the natural sciences and medicine.
The series is edited by Martin Döring and Jörg Niewöhner.

Advisory Board:
Prof. Dr. Thomas Lemke, Prof. Dr. Paul Martin, Prof. Dr. Brigitte Nerlich, Prof. Dr. John Law, Prof. Dr. Regine Kollek, Prof. Dr. Allan Young

Ariane d'Hoop trained as a stage designer, studied spatial arrangements in performing arts and then completed a joint PhD in architecture (Université Libre de Bruxelles) and anthropology (University of Amsterdam). She has developed a microethnographic attention to the materiality of places, most of them in Brussels, to explore how it matters in situated social practices.

Ariane d'Hoop

The Slightest Attachment

When Psychiatric Spaces Enact Affinities

[transcript]

This book derives from a doctoral research. The study was funded by a scholarship from the Fonds de la Recherche Scientifique (F.R.S.-FNRS, grant ID: 11056514), and its finalization was supported by the Fonds Alice et David van Buuren. The thesis was titled *Modest Attachments. An Inquiry into the Potentialities of Material Spaces in a Psychiatric Day Care Centre* (2018, Université de Bruxelles & University of Amsterdam).

This Book was then published with the financial support of the FRS-FNRS. The publication also received funding from the Centre de recherches et d'interventions sociologiques (CESIR), Universite Saint-Louis – Bruxelles (Belgium); from the department of Ethics, Law & Medical Humanities, Amsterdam Universiteit Medische Centra (UMC), University of Amsterdam, my employer at the time of writing; from the Health, Care and the Body Programme Group at the Amsterdam Institute for Social Science Research (AISSR), University of Amsterdam; and from the FWO-WOG Belgian Science and Technology in Society (BSTS), KU Leuven, Belgium.

Bibliographic information published by the Deutsche Nationalbibliothek
The Deutsche Nationalbibliothek lists this publication in the Deutsche Nationalbibliografie; detailed bibliographic data are available in the Internet at http://dnb.d-nb.de

First published in 2023 by transcript Verlag, Bielefeld
© Ariane d'Hoop

Cover concept: Kordula Röckenhaus, Bielefeld
Printed by: Majuskel Medienproduktion GmbH, Wetzlar
https://doi.org/10.14361/9783839465561
Print-ISBN 978-3-8376-6556-7
PDF-ISBN 978-3-8394-6556-1
ISSN of series: 2751-2878
eISSN of series: 2751-2886

Printed on permanent acid-free text paper.

To Blanche Beaujeant

Contents

Table of Figures

All photographs and drawings are by the author, except where otherwise indicated. On hand-drawn maps, symbols of furniture, people, or things refer to standard figures in architectural drawing.

Acknowledgments

First a research for the setting of a theater play, then a doctoral dissertation, and now a book, this project has spanned a decade. It is thus not surprising that many people have contributed to this book along the road of its creation. First of all, I dearly thank Jeannette Pols for her invaluable support. Her scholarship and friendship continue to inspire me, and I feel warmly grateful for our ongoing collaboration.

It gives me great pleasure to thank all the caregivers, patients, architects, and employees of psychiatric facilities, who allowed me to spend time with them and generously answered my questions. All nourished this work while welcoming its search deep into the details of their practices and things. Special thanks are owing to Evelyne Chambeau, Bastien Paternotte, and to the team of the Centre de Jour pour Adolescents. The unique, vibrant atmosphere that they created there has infused the very substance of this study.

I would also like to thank the members of the academic communities that have offered intellectual stimulation over the years that this work has been taking shape. Some of them supported the project in its early stages. Thank you to Vinciane Despret, Laurent Legrain, and Michael Ghyoot. Thanks go most profoundly to Benedikte Zitouni for her ongoing support. I am grateful to all the people who have listened and engaged with my ideas: to members of the research lab Sasha at the Faculté d'Architecture at the Université Libre de Bruxelles; to Julien Pieron and the participants in the workshops of 'Fructis – Contemporary politics of nature' in the department of Philosophy at the Université de Liège; to members of the GECo (Groupe d'Études Constructivistes) who organized the colloquium called 'Gestes spéculatifs' in the castle of Cerisy; to the friends and colleagues of the research and reading group P3G; to those of the Department of Anthropology and of the 'AMC philosophy of care meetings' at the University of Amsterdam. Special thanks to the friends, colleagues and jury members who have read and discussed earlier versions of the chapters: Tanja Ahlin, Filippo Bertoni, Gideon Boie, Isabelle Doucet, Annelieke Driessen, Thierry Drumm, Antoine Hennion, Lisette Jong, Kristine Krause, Justine Laurent, Pauline Lefevbre, Swasti Mishra, Annemarie Mol, Nicolas Prignot, Christine Schaut, Wakana Suzuki, François Thoreau, Mattijs Van de Port, Else Vogel, Dick Willems. Our exchanges pervaded my mind with thinking and enthusiasm. To say the least, I have learned a great deal from working with you all.

During the researching and writing of this book, I was fortunate to receive financial supports. The research was funded by a scholarship from the Fonds de la Recherche Scientifique (F.R.S.—FNRS, grant ID: 11056514), and its finalization was supported by the Fonds Alice et David Van Buuren. I am thankful to my colleagues of the Center for Sociological Intervention & Research (CESIR) at the Université Saint-Louis – Bruxelles, and to the Belgian Science, Technology and Society Network (B.STS), for supporting the publication of this book. Thank you to Jakob Horstmann and Luisa Bott at transcript Publishing for their editorial guidance, to the anonymous reviewers for their constructive critiques, and to Jörg Niewöhner and his co-editors for welcoming the book in their series. Thanks as well to Erin Martineau and Emily Darrow who corrected the English of several versions.

Last but not least, a number of comrades encouraged, shared ideas, hence making it possible to carry this out over years. Thank you to Didier Demorcy, Gregory d'Hoop, Robert Doane, Claire Farah, Maarten Gielen, Benjamin Lasserre, Elsa Maury, Olivia Mengue, Isabelle Rousseau, Sylvie Somville, and Karolina Svobodova. I need to thank my family for all their support and patience, especially my dear Thierry Drumm, my mother Bernadette Smeesters, and my grandmother Blanche Beaujeant. I dedicate this book to her.

Preface

There are three main ways in which 'space' is considered in mental health care and policy – and in other care settings, too. The first is in terms of 'regional space'. In the context of long-term mental health care, regional metaphors frame care institutions as existing 'outside' society. Psychiatric hospitals started booming in the western world at the turn of the 20th century. They represented a therapeutic optimism and a medical approach that aimed to cure people suffering from severe mental health problems. When this optimism gradually proved wrong, patients got stuck in these institutions.

Over the course of the 20th century, psychiatric hospitals were increasingly seen as disciplinary spaces and asylums rather than places for treatment. This is a second way of thinking about space, alongside geographic location. Quality of care was questioned both from outside and from within the profession. The critique as well as the demand for change used metaphors of regional and disciplinary space to orient themselves. Patients were seen as physically excluded from society, and treated as 'inmates' rather than patients. They had to reintegrate in society, to become citizens among other citizens.

The third way of thinking about space in long-term mental health care is closely related to this thinking about citizenship and what it means to be part of society. It is about the space around a citizen. Citizens are then seen as autonomous beings, who should be left with enough space around them to make their own decisions about their lives. This space for autonomy is not merely metaphorical. Its practical implications are to guarantee people their freedom to not be disciplined by institutions, and to allow them to do whatever they want, as long as they are not obstructing the freedom of others. The ideal of citizenship requires a policy of leaving people alone.

A lot has been written about deinstitutionalization and citizenship for the disenfranchized, but this book adds an original angle to the debate. Ariane d'Hoop carefully explores how the *material space* in a care practice for teenagers with mental health problems is actively involved in their care. The notion of material space may sound counter-intuitive when thinking in terms of regional space, or may evoke images of a panopticon where the materiality of buildings adds to the disciplining of 'inmates'. However, by foregrounding the materiality of concrete buildings and the 'stuff' within them, d'Hoop provides new angles from which we can understand spaces, their materiality, and their inhabitants. The book takes us on a fascinating ethnographic journey to show how caregivers make the material space of the building of the day center part of the teens' care. This space does not emerge in the book as disciplinary space (although there are these kinds of spaces, too), nor as a place to move away from, nor a *tabula rasa* for these stranded young people to shape. The author analyzes the material space as *potentialities*: invitations or possibilities for doing things. These can be affordances, suggestions or more explicit proposals meant to materially evoke what these young people like, what they are interested in and how they may be enabled to live together. Even the most subtle cues (a nice painting, a spot that is 'chill' for hanging out) may provoke an interest or possibility to explore.

In line with the therapeutic vision of the caregivers, invitations honor peoples' preferences, but may also be rejected or ignored, failing to engage someone. The space does not *determine* what happens. Hence, the author paints a picture of subtle interactions, of small seductions, of persistent and shifting laps of support for interests, and of temporary or failing relationships. Her analysis shows how material space and social environment open a range of possibilities for people to respond to their invitations in their own ways.

The analysis of these subtle workings of inviting material spaces is thought-provoking to providers of mental health care and of other forms of care in communities. Moving 'psychiatric space' away from institutional buildings and into patients' homes and appointment offices cuts off many repertoires for helping young people with mental health problems recover. Inventive forms of institutional space provide patients with invitations to find ways of life marked not only by attempts to contain tumultuous family life, the management of psychiatric problems or failure at school, but also by the things they enjoy, find interesting or want to explore. This is an urgent call in times of deinstitutionalizing mental health care.

The insights from this book are, however, not restricted to the particular mental health care buildings analyzed in the book. Her analysis invites readers to think about care for and through space in other places, too. How is the architecture of public spaces inviting people to act? How does this happen in teaching situations, in cultural centers, or in municipalities that increasingly use digital means for communicating with its citizens? What actions do public spaces invite, what ways of acting do they make possible, what do they forbid, who do they reject? The book fuels imaginative reflections about these questions, not in terms of "letting the individual decide to leave or not" nor of "how social order may be enforced", but in terms of imagining what public spaces may afford, invite, and make possible. This is a relevant and urgent call at a time when our common way of materially and socially living together is challenged by pandemics and environmental problems. The book makes clear that material spaces act. The question is not how to keep them from doing this, but how they may act in the best possible ways.

Weesp, January 2022
Jeannette Pols

Chapter 1
Introduction

In an urban area of Brussels, under the doorbell of a banal domestic townhouse, a small label declared the building a 'Day Center for Teenagers' (figure 1). Had someone rung the bell, a youth or adult wearing casual clothes would come to open the door. Or the secretary might poke her head out her first-floor window to see who had arrived, instead of using the intercom. Once past the threshold, newcomers would enter a vestibule where they would notice intensive traces of wear and hear the creaking of the floorboards above. After a few steps, they would find a small staircase, whose doors gave access to a living room, or to a dining room open to a kitchen and a yard. There, they would come upon people sitting or leaning against a table, addressing each other by their first names while they chatted about the daily news and shared their opinions. Some would sip at cups of coffee and, if it was late morning, they'd smell a meal being prepared. Such visits would have most likely occurred until 2014. That year, the day center moved to a new building located a few streets from the townhouse. The new place was an existing building on a much bigger site, freshly redesigned (figure 2). The name of the center was visible on its façade, without indicating that the teens were diagnosed with psychiatric disorders. At the entrance, large windows opened onto a view of the secretary who could see the visitors and open the door to let them in with a remote control. Newcomers who entered found a waiting area at the start of a long corridor. For them to reach the core of the day center, where caregivers and teens shared daily life, they had to walk down that corridor, pass another door, then another corridor that led to the caregivers' office, after which stood the living spaces.

The differences between the entrances of the old house and the new building were small, but important. These spatial modifications induced caregiving in utterly different ways. This psychiatric day center for teenagers initially inherited the 'therapeutic community' model, in which everyone present in the center takes part in its everyday organization and social life. Although the center had made room for biomedical psychiatry about ten years earlier, when moving to the new location, the sharing of informal and ordinary moments of everyday life continued to be crucial to their care work. The old town house incorporated the values that have been constitutive of community psychiatry for decades. Its anonymous façade and public entrance avoided stigmatization of its occupants. Not only did it avoid displaying the psychiatric troubles that brought them there, but it also dismissed the idea that these troubles should be addressed by the disciplinary order of traditional institutions, such as hospitals, schools, or other welfare settings. Once inside, the building's domestic layout encouraged direct immersion and informality. As for the entrance of the new building, it induced quite different interactions with the space and between its users. The display of a logo, the glass entrance with its view of a secretarial office, the remote-controlled doors, the waiting room and corridors, all made palpable that this was a professional place primarily devoted to treatment.

These changes were far from trivial. The new entrance especially raised problems about the role of the secretary, who was not intended to be a hostess or, worse, a gatekeeper. Instead, she had to remain immersed in the everyday events of the group with the other caregivers and the teens. The team attempted to retain that sense of immersion for her. Details of her office arrangements then became of greater importance: her desk remained a large working table with chairs on both sides, rather than a higher, formal receptionist's desk with a counter. Plus, after moving to the new location, the caregivers and teens took care to involve the secretary's space in the group's daily life by often stopping by for a chat. The new entrance layout required effort to maintain these casual interactions with teens that the caregivers deemed elementary in their work.

Matters of space

This book is an ethnographic study of the spatial arrangements in a care institution. It takes us into a specific place, the psychiatric day center for teenagers I introduced a moment ago, to better understand how a building and its interior spaces contribute to everyday care. This care center offers a specific entry for such an exploration because it speaks to significant changes that have been transforming the psychiatric field over the last fifty years. These changes entail a profound, ongoing questioning and reconfiguration of what a care institution might be. In terms of spaces, the most remarkable change across the diverse movements that established community psychiatry lies in the implementation of small facilities in houses outside hospital walls and their disciplinary organization. Yet these places were not only different due to their insertion in streets and neighborhoods. The materiality of the houses, their room layouts, and their disposition of furniture and objects also made a world of difference for the patients' daily experience of care. The original premise of my research is that there is a lot to learn from the spatial arrangements of such community facilities and from their usages. They offer insights not only to researchers and practitioners interested in psychiatric settings, but also into the spatial organization of other care institutions such as youth centers, group homes, or even nursing homes or schools, with respect to their specificities and differences. My hope is that you, the reader, will better perceive how material spaces subtly contribute to or hinder care after closing the book.

Certainly, that psychiatric day center can teach us about spaces of care, since its heritage carries a vivid reflection on institutional life. But it also deserves a closer examination, amid many other facilities I visited, because its move to a new building brought to the surface many matters of space that spanned concerns of caregivers, teenagers, architects, medical and administrative directors, and mine. The design project aimed at providing caregivers and teens better conditions for their practice, while maintaining what was already working for them in the old house. Until then, in their ongoing care work, matters of space had always implicitly been diluted by other flows of concerns. As perhaps goes without saying, those concerns usually centered on the patients. But the transition created a rupture from a place populated by implicit habits, meaningful stories and histories, a place that required ingenuity when coping with inconveniences. This rupture raised the question, for both the caregivers and the teens, of how to retrieve what had rendered the original location so specific to them. Therefore, the transition required the caregivers to formulate the specific values and details of their spaces, to convey them to architects and directors. Each of us needed to learn about matters of space, although for different purposes.

As an anthropologist, my purpose is to relay what has been learned both from that transition and my ethnographic exploration of the everyday practice in that center, and to articulate these stories in order to bring novel insights about institutional spaces of care. In care ethnographies, at the crossroad of medical anthropology and studies of sciences and technology, I found research techniques and conceptual tools enabling a close look at spatial arrangements. These techniques and tools enabled me to probe how the materiality of spaces *works* in the care practice. Just as the story about the new entrance would lead us to suspect, spatial arrangements must be considered in how they induce everyday interactions and values in care situations, while none of these ingredients alone fully determine the others. The entrance story invites us to venture further into the building, guided by these questions: What do material spaces enable caregivers and teens to do? How do these tangible arrangements make them act? When do they succeed or fail? What tensions or contradictions do they generate? And, in turn, what does 'care' become when analyzed through a spatial lens?

This book offers some answers to these questions by bringing into view how specific spatial arrangements and their usages carry a form of care that has to do with the formation of patients' attachments. It recounts how material spaces, together with caregiving techniques, provide subtle conditions to bring out teenagers' affinities, even from their slightest degree of existence. These community-based care practices and their spaces are critical in today's institutional landscape. They are all too often unrecognized, disqualified by biomedical knowledge, if not already devastated by the shifting landscape of deinstitutionalization and its discourses on management. By describing how matters of space are enacted in practice, this book invokes a further reflection on 'responsive care', namely, how caregivers' attentiveness to small and contingent occurrences gives room to what moves teenagers, to what matters to them. Before turning to this community care and the link I draw with the idea of attachment and its implications, I would like to describe how I studied the spaces in this research.

Figure 1: The old town house (2013).

Figure 2: The new building (2014).

An ethnographic take

This book follows the contours of *material spaces*. But what is a study of spatial arrangements? And how to look at these arrangements in relation to care? I started to pay closer attention to spaces when I was a scenographer. Although my work involved the drawing of plans, the building of models, and a certain knowledge of materials and construction techniques, the creation of theatre and exhibition sets induced another relationship to spatial design than that of architects. This became obvious when I started looking for monographs on contemporary psychiatric buildings, and found them on the shelves of architecture libraries. In these books, I could see drawings, wide-angled photographs, and maps of architectural projects (Kovess-Masféty et al. 2004; Mens & Wagenaar 2010: 239–245; Laget, Laroche & Duhau (2016 [2012]): 459–471, 504–508). People were rarely depicted in them. Reading on, I learned about the themes that traversed these design projects. Buildings should look as 'normal' (that is, as non-medical) as possible. They incorporate arrangements for sociability. And prevention of aggression against oneself and others may also be considered. While these books allowed me to pinpoint recurring themes, my background as a scenographer prompted me to further understand how these spaces interfered with the dynamics of care as they played out in situations I observed.[1] Indeed, architects are trained to focus on design projects and seldom on post-delivery uses, while scenographers continue to modify stage sets throughout the rehearsal process. It is only when actresses and actors play with a set that we can observe if a scene works or not, and this process often demands modifications along the way. Consequently, I could hardly reduce my perspective to the conception of buildings and the themes inscribed in these spaces. I came to consider the ways in which they change over time, while being transformed in accordance with users' practices.

What's more, while moving my scenographer's gaze onto academic research, it was no surprise that it found its best translation in micro-ethnography. Rather than embracing an entire building, what fell under scrutiny were the spatial arrangements or elements with which occupants interacted.[2] In this way, the descriptions in this book go into

---

1   Note that geographers have also developed an interest in the spatiality of 'mental health' facilities. Rather than putting the materiality of buildings *per se* under the lens, they focus on mapping locations of care settings, distributions of people with mental disorders, as well as the significance of place for the patients. See Wolch & Philo (2000) for an overview.

2   For works that also put material spaces under the magnifying glass, and develop interactional perspectives on them, see Koolhaas & colleagues' (2014) robust monographic series about the 'architectural elements' that constitute a building (windows, ceilings, stairs, heating, etc.); the book *Usus/usures. État des lieux – How things stand* (Rotor, d'Hoop & Zitouni 2010) that renews an interest

the detail of interactions with the materiality of the spaces of the day center for teens. From Goffman's (1963; 1971) depictions of encounters in public places, I learned to seriously consider what can be at stake in people's interactions through their mutual, verbal and non-verbal responses.[3] Therefore, in this book, the 'material spaces' are the matter and texture with which one can interact in tactile and meaningful ways. They can take the shape of a room, a corner, a furniture element, or any other thing. I trace everyday interactions with the day center's tangible environment, as caregivers and teens move, sit, adjust their distance, establish eye contact, adjust their body position, orient themselves, pay attention to their surroundings, wander around them, touch them, manipulate things and display others, distribute their presence and, over longer periods of time, vary the spatial arrangements.

Therefore, if spaces are indissociable from interactions with them, how to understand the activity at hand? Goffman argues that spaces are not 'out there', external to people's interactions, and stresses the varying normativity of places (such as differing expectations for interacting in a restaurant versus a bedroom). Yet his works "built on a vision of space as a resource ready and waiting to be mobilized by conscious human agents" (Prior 1988: 89). Latour (1996 [1994]), following in interactionists' footsteps, tackles this problem. He calls for us to pay close attention to scenes of interaction equipped with objects, clothes, designed places, etc., by describing how they contribute to shaping actions. In other words, he contends that objects are delegated "to both replace human action and constrain and shape the actions of other humans" (Latour 2008: 151). In the care center, this means that material spaces make care-

---

in architecture about the wear of materials, uses, users and construction practices; and see also Conein, Dodier & Thévenot (1993) for a collection of studies about people's engagement with objects in practices, beyond analyses of them as tools or symbols.

3   However, I do not share Goffman's aim in bringing up the acting out of social norms and the exclusion they delineate. In my fieldwork, these norms appeared much more indeterminate. Teens' behavior that failed to match social expectations could open opportunities to shake the local normativity (d'Hoop 2021a).

givers and care receivers act in particular ways. Each spatial element and human being plays a respective role as an actor in its encounters.

The materiality of care

A body of works has prolonged this ethnographic invitation to describe the agency of materiality on health and social care terrains. These authors investigate what constitutes "care in practice", as Mol, Moser and Pols (2010) titled a representative collection. They recount how care is *done* empirically, with its techniques, ways of doing, materiality, and events, and they conceptualize through these descriptions.[4] These care studies hold a particular view on things and technologies in care work. They cultivate a 'material semiotic' approach, meaning that they refuse to separate *a priori* the material world from that of ideas. In this approach, material objects do not reflect, represent or symbolize ideas, meanings, or values that people attribute to them. Instead, these studies contend that ideas take shape in and with the material world in ongoing practices.[5] They thus explore the relationships that weave between people and materialities, like technology or things, as well as what those relationships produce in an ongoing practice.[6] Think, for instance, of the modes of entanglement that take shape between wheelchair and

---

4   I can hardly encapsulate in one note the scope of studies that align with this approach. Those relevant for this research punctuate the book. Note, too, that in the fields of medical anthropology and nursing studies, many works have focused on practices as well, yet without articulating the active role of materiality. For a recent publication that discusses the approaches to the materiality of care, such as clothing or waiting rooms, see Buse, Martin & Nettleton (2018).

5   Nord and Högström (2017) provide a collection of studies about the architecture of care institutions (in the UK and Scotland) through a closely similar approach, which they label "non-representational theory" (10).

6   The material-semiotic approach does not posit foundational explanations. It gives descriptive details about how relations assemble or dissociate between humans and other beings. They do not propose general theories; these studies emphasize their situatedness as well as the transport of the knowledge they carry. For one account about material semiotics, see Law (2009).

the person it hosts (Winance 2019); or of the effects of telecare devices on how patients and nurses address problems, invent new routines, acquire knowledge, and form new webs of interdependence (Pols 2012).

In this view, the good, bad or ambivalent values at stake in care situations are not located in human minds and projected on neutral objects. Instead, these values pervade technologies, things, local strivings, routines, the application or shifting of rules, or the know-how particular to a practice.[7] Or, to put it another way, the values that matter in a care practice are neither subjective nor objective, neither universal nor essential, but they are dynamic within the specific situations where people and things interact (Pols 2015). The values and concerns embedded in the spatial surroundings animate everyday care practice. Therefore, in this book, I bring out how interactions with the spaces of the day center contribute to the emergence of attachments: when teens develop affinities as caregivers attempt to elicit them through mediation of the material environment.

Ultimately, I see the worth of these empirical care studies in their inheritance of pragmatic philosophy. They tell us about ways of doing and materialities that are not permanent, but involve persistent experimentation as caregivers attempt to improve the problematic situations they deal with. Rather than taking a strict critical posture, describing experimentation starts instead from the assumption that practitioners try to develop a good practice, or the best possible practice, without ignoring tricky aspects. This posture does not claim that objects and technologies can solve ethical issues, but rather shows how they cast these issues into sharper relief. In the practice of adjusting and continual experimenting, things and technologies, too, are 'attuned' (Mol 2008: 55; Mol, Moser & Pols 2010: 7–25).[8] In contrast to analyses that assign explanations to ex-

---

7   This empirical approach to care, then, differs from traditional care ethics because what care is, and what is good or bad within it, is not defined according to researchers' prescriptive criteria, but after having conducted situated inquiries and articulated them (Pols 2015).

8   Other ethnographies of care in non-Western hospitals have shown how improvisation is vital as well in biomedical practices (Street 2012; Livingstone 2012). Although adopting different conceptual frameworks, in medical anthropology

ternal forces or greater structures, such empirical care studies compel us as theorists to leave the protective shell of grand determinations, and to try to better report on and respond to situations that can hardly be limited by such certainties. The ethnography of spaces in care practices allows us to make visible how these arrangements are in turn involved in attentive experimentations, without deterministic or causal pretension. This non-deterministic view sidesteps a tale of the 'spatial influence' on users. Rather than merely impacting how caregivers and teens act, the spaces of the day center enact potentialities that open paths for their actions in ways that are unpredictable, but nonetheless consequential for the care work and its place (d'Hoop 2021b).[9]

In this sense, this ethnography of a building also adds a stone to architectural studies that are concerned with situated, embodied accounts of buildings and spatial arrangements (Doucet & Frichot 2018). These studies seek to resist a vision of architecture that claims to be autonomous, that is, supposedly disentangled from particular places, things, and people's lives.[10] There is indeed a strong tradition

---

the subfield of hospital ethnography carves a path for microanalyses of various institutional lives in both social and professional aspects. Insights into this evolving specialty can be found in Long, Hunter & van der Geest (2008); Finkler, Hunter & Iedema (2008); and Street & Coleman (2012). The latter brings into focus the multiple spatial orderings, biomedical and others, at play in hospitals.

9   I can thus observe, as an ethnographer, how the spaces may enact or not teens' affinities in the daily care practice. The concept of 'enactment' puts the practice in question at the core of the inquiry: it is about the material and social activity that generates realities in practices (Mol 2002). This concept undertakes an ontological point: "If an object is real this is because it is part of a practice. It is a reality *enacted*." (44, original emphasis).

10   Most of these authors find a primary interest in the architects' design practices (for instance, Yaneva 2009a, or Houdart 2009), but they may also observe how actual spaces induce certain uses and social relations as Yenava (2009b) does with staircases, doors and conference rooms. According to Martin et al. (2015), an adequate social study of healthcare architecture demands exploring buildings both through their construction project and their experience by users.

in the architectural discipline that conceives buildings as the prestigious artworks of designers, drawn on white pages, and then built on
empty sites. This framework excludes any counter-narrative that would
welcome more marginal actors – such as existing lands, mundane
infrastructures, or users and their words, practices and concerns. Of
course, critiques within the architectural field have been calling for a
greater sensitivity to users and their uses of spaces (Blundell Jones,
Petrescu & Till 2005; Cupers 2013; Doucet 2015: 111–132). What ethnography can offer, then, is a fine-tuned description of how a specific material
environment and its usage take shape, and with whom, and, over time,
how they undergo necessary changes. I hope that such a situated account enables us to unravel the potential of an institutional place that is
inhabited and arranged with care, and hence, to better perceive what it
could be.[11]

The day center

The day center for teens belonged to an institution called *L'Équipe* that
was created in 1964 as one of the precursors of the deinstitutionalization
movement in Brussels. Its first facility was established in relation to
Brugmann, a hospital affiliated with the Université Libre de Bruxelles.
The aim was to move patients from its psychiatric unit and to host them
in a 'therapeutic community'.[12] This care model is based on the idea that
everyone present in the center takes part in its organization and social
life, especially through mundane daily interactions such as sharing a
meal, moving about, or improvising a chat. This was to help participants

11   On this speculative posture, that is, a posture that explores the transformative
      potentials of situated, empirical inquiries, their narrations, and relational per-
      spectives, see Debaise & Stengers (2015). On the inspiration from this posture
      in architectural studies, Doucet, Debaise & Zitouni (2018).
12   The names of all facilities are real but, on their request, all the names of my
      interlocutors are pseudonyms. Majerus (2013) offers a micro-history of spatial
      organization in the Brugmann hospital (34–83), and of Brussels' context when
      shifting to community facilities, including to L'Équipe (ibid: 257–286).

learn how to better deal with their feelings and with the impacts of social interactions, as well as further consolidating their personalities.[13] During the five next decades, L'Équipe expanded into 19 other buildings, all located in urban areas. They included eight other centers, the location of the administrative and maintenance staff, a library, an art gallery, and ateliers. The day center for teenagers was created in the early 2000s. Since then, it has been hosting teens (aged 12–18) diagnosed with different kinds of disorder. All of them were school dropouts. When I joined them, more than half of the teens were sent by psychiatric units, most of them by mental health workers, and some by the juvenile justice court, youth welfare services, or their parents. A few of them were living in welfare institutions. In the day center's neighborhood, caregivers and youths regularly frequented public facilities, a park, bakeries, supermarkets, local shopping streets, a swimming pool, or the district library (figure 3).

At the time of my research, the team was still practicing the initial community model. The institution still worked in collaboration with Brugmann, where the medical director was based and from which she sometimes sent teens. The caregivers of the day center called their work "sociotherapy" and also referred to "institutional psychotherapy".[14] Baptiste, the coordinator, teamed up with five educators, three social workers, two artists, two psychologists, three nurses, two psychiatrists, a secretary, temporary external artists or trainees, and a medical director who came once a week as clinical staff. Besides the doctors, all

---

13   An initial reference in this school of thought is Jones (1953). For secondary sources: Fussinger (2011) provides a historical report of therapeutic communities; Spandler (2006) draws lessons from a historical case study (in the UK) for today's and tomorrow's social actions; and Smith and Spitzmueller (2016) give an ethnographic account of such a 'milieu therapy' from the caregivers' perspective.

14   The basic assumption of this French movement is that caring for people is done by caring for the institution. A vast literature has been written about it. For historical documents that offer in-depth reflections on the spatial dimensions of Institutional Therapy, see Guattari (1967); Murard & Fourquet (1975). For a philosophical reading of its therapeutic practice, see Rozier (2014).

members of the team were "sociotherapists". They came to know the teens by sharing a daily life filled with informal moments in living spaces (*le communautaire*) and diverse places for activities. Weekly community meetings gathered all the teenagers and some of the caregivers. Each of them was invited to bring issues they wanted to discuss. Relationships, or rather the conditions of togetherness in the center, were often dissected under a microscope during these meetings. Another important aspect of this care work was its opening to the external world by going outside, or by bringing experiences, things, or people from outside into the center.

As years have passed, the team has come to combine this community life with analytical work, inspired by psychoanalysis and systemic approaches.[15] Next to an individual focus, they considered patients' relationships and interactional dynamics in the group and with their own relatives (Vermeylen & Schouters-Decroly 2001). Since 2005, the care practice also integrated a biomedical approach. The caregivers were at first very skeptical about the inclusion of a nurses' office in the center, with its medicine cabinet and prescriptions. But they eventually accepted the biomedical work, provided that medication was used at the minimum necessary level. This was noticeable in the spatial organization as well. In both the old house and the new building, the living spaces and workshop rooms were located at the core. The infirmary was deliberately set back with the consultation rooms on the upper floors, unlike hospital wards where the nurses' station is often central (figures 4a-d; figures 5a-c).

That combination of community work and both psychodynamic and biomedical approaches, it must be said, remained under debate in the ongoing practice. The differences between these frameworks were especially strained when they implied a hierarchy of knowledge about patients, and even more so when a decision about treatment involved un-

---

15   Though psychoanalysis mostly took place in conversations in consultation offices, its influence in the community work manifested when caregivers gave importance to what the teenagers said. Speech was a valued ingredient to better understand them.

certainty. This was the case with Samira. When she arrived in the center, she had been prescribed a high dose of Zyprexa, a medication used for schizophrenia. But after two months, the sociotherapists gave a report that cast doubts on that diagnosis, highlighting her intellectual vivacity in workshops, bodily attitude, relationship to her mother, and school reports. After having listened to the portrait presented by the team, the medical director rethought the diagnosis and changed Samira's medication to a much less strong one. That was a risky choice. The caregivers cautioned that they should all be attentive to Samira's response to this change.

Their decision involved a crucial process of craft: when caregivers were unsure of the way to continue with a youth, they used their different ways of knowing to address the issue. The team jointly composed a portrait of each youth. Day after day, they built an informal knowledge of the teens, notably by testing each of their responses with like and dislike. They revisited and refined this knowledge time and again, meeting after meeting. Tensions became palpable, though, when psychiatrists used their scientific knowledge in a way that silenced other caregivers' reports. But the story of Samira shows that it did not always happen that way. The complex portraits of each teenager that the team created enabled them to take careful decisions about treatment, whether it concerned medication or non-biomedical therapeutic propositions. Nothing less is at stake in how ordinary spaces help create mundane affinities, than what knowledge and which therapeutic possibilities can be explored in the course of care work.

Figure 3: The neighborhood of the day center.

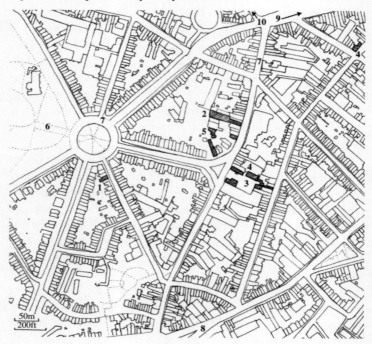

1 The old house
2 The new building
3 Administrative and maintenance staff, art gallery and library of the institution
4 Others centers and ateliers of the institution
5 Clay Atelier
6 Park
7 Bakeries
8 Supermarket
9 Shopping street
10 Public library and swimming pool

Figure 4a: The basement of the old house.

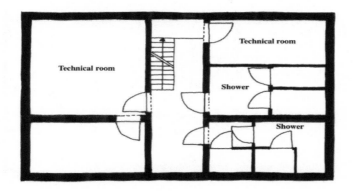

Figure 4b: The ground floor of the old house.

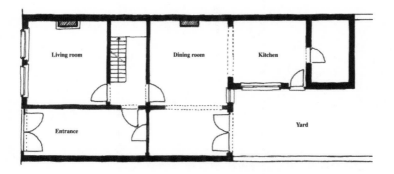

Figure 4c: The first floor of the old house.

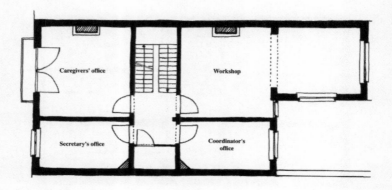

Figure 4d: The second floor of the old house.

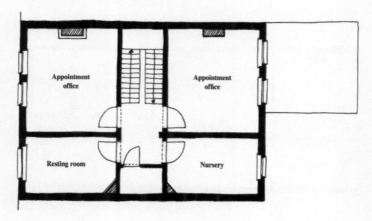

Figure 5a-c: The basement (top), ground floor (middle) and first floor (bottom) of the new building.

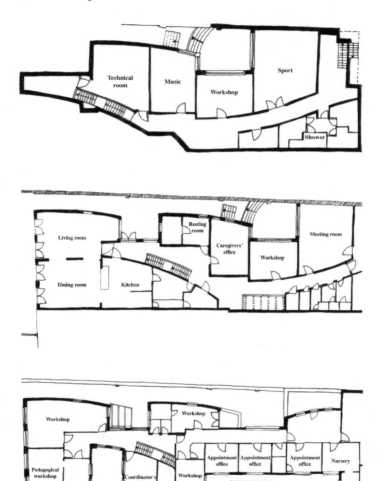

Slight attachments

The psychiatric day center for teens had a very special atmosphere. I was impressed by how, each time I was back, I felt caught up so quickly in its dynamic current, where everyone was intermingling and shared a set of concerns. "This place doesn't convey distress", I thought, comparing it to other stark settings, permeated with neglect and desolation, that I had visited elsewhere or read about (Rhodes 1991: 11–33). Of course, this place and its small community weren't intended to host acute crises, nor was its people exempt from suffering or tensions. But rather than reminding people of their own deficiencies, they seemed to succeed in bringing forth specific aspects of patients' personalities – what they liked or disfavored, their ways of interacting, their interests – through which each of them could experiment with who they could be. If that place related to care, it was through the creation of such affinities.

I learned to identify these affinities as attachments by reading the work of Antoine Hennion. For a little over two decades, together with his colleagues of the *Centre de Sociologie de l'Innovation* (Paris), Hennion (2017) has given a renewed and fertile meaning to the notion of 'attachment'. He seeks to understand the formation of passion: how does it happen that people come to strongly like something? As a French pragmatic sociologist, his challenge is to conceptualize how people develop tastes in practice, and how they become more and more sensitive to objects, which in turn gain finely delineated differences.[16] Gomart and Hennion (1999) proposed to speak of 'attachment' after having interviewed music lovers and drug users. Their interlocutors described how they completely gave themselves up to the constraints of sophisticated practices, like attending a rock concert or preparing a pipe for a crack high, and forged their sensitivities along with these techniques, objects, and collectives.

---

16   In the field of sociology of art, the focus on practices overtakes Bourdieu's critical view (social determinism), and distinguishes itself from sociologists who speak of beliefs, even when they closely describe experiences of tasting (such as Howard Becker's conventions). See Hennion (2004: 23).

In these studies on taste, when someone gets attached, it implies assessment conducted within a situation, during moments of attention where the qualities of an object unfold together with the person and body that comes to feel it. These moments of attention, Hennion and Teil (2004) detail about wine lovers, occur for instance when a guest at a dinner takes his glass of wine, drinks a small amount, stops for an instant, inhales, drinks again, slightly moves his lips, and sinks back into the flow of conversation. But the formation of attachment to objects goes beyond those acts of paying attention. They also entail the weaving together of a collective of people with whom taste is shared and debated. To develop a taste for something requires retrying the trial, questioning the object again. In this way, amateurs' sensitivities are revised, refined, and consolidated. Attachment, in this socio-pragmatic perspective, thus refers to the processes along which a person or group comes to hold on to things that hold them in return. When these affinities manifest, they entail the objects' feedback, bodily engagements, sensations, situations with their material devices, and collectives of people (Hennion 2005). Therefore, this notion allows us to describe how sensitivities come into being in situated practices, where the material equipment plays mediating roles in the way an attachment takes shape.[17]

---

17   The idea of 'mediation' helps the concept of attachment to blur traditional dua-
      lisms. In a nutshell, Hennion's concept of attachment draws inspiration to the
      Actor-Network Theory: after the object-as-network, it theorizes the subject-as-
      network. This implies that subjects are acted upon by objects as much as they
      activate their state of passion. Hence the concept of attachment renders it im-
      possible to maintain oppositions between free agents or people determined by
      structures; between activity or passivity; or between a causality attributed eit-
      her to a subject or to an object. Instead, as the stories in this book will reiterate,
      the attention paid to attachments traces a *middle path* where no one is active or
      passive, free or alienated. In this tale, material spaces do not hold by themsel-
      ves, in their shape or substance, the power to create attachment. Instead they
      contribute to making an appreciation happen as mediators (among a chain of
      many mediators, like rehearsals, habits, rules, etc.) that stabilize, question, or
      transform the relationship between artworks and their passionate lovers over
      time (Hennion 2015 [1993]).

However, the affinities that I came to discern in the day center were, for the most part, not exactly passions enacted with great dedication. Most of these affinities were more modest and tenuous. They were less intense and less stable. They emerged from smaller things being liked, but diluted in the mundane flow of daily life, for only a few of these attachments grew more strongly. Teens became attached through familiar bonds in living spaces (chapter two), or ephemeral involvements in workshops (chapter three). Their likes and dislikes took shape when they responded to invitations from their environment, such as a corner to withdraw in, the smell of a dinner, or an inspiring artwork. Their attachments did not especially concern the place or its occupants, but anything else that a teen may come to like. Over time, some of these inclinations developed from everyday banality to long-lasting interests (chapter four), as when a fashion craze swept over a bunch of them. These interests, once shared within the group, led to new activities, and hence to the rearrangement of spaces. The institutional place then became 'lively', being animated by the temporal dynamics of those attachments (chapter five).

The idea that attachments are not always dearly cherished is not, in itself, a major discovery. Hennion already suspects that his descriptions resonate beyond the amateurs' techniques to get into peak condition and great sensations:

> Why not generalize this analysis of the amateur's competencies to far more varied forms of attachment? Can the amateur's meticulous, highly elaborate, debated knowledge not provide a model for analyzing more ordinary, lay, silent devices through which we are (and make ourselves be) present to the situations in which we live, throughout the day? What great amateurs enable us to see more easily, owing to their high level of engagement in a particular practice, is a range of social techniques that make us able to produce and continuously to adjust a creative relationship with objects, with others, with ourselves and with our bodies; in other words, a pragmatic presence vis-à-vis the world that makes us and that we make. (Hennion 2005: 142)

The important insight here is that many attachments may well be at stake in the ordinary techniques and devices that moderately enliven our everyday states. This insight opens our view on a far wider range of engagements with the things we hold on to in daily life. These seemingly mundane attachments in fact remain sensitive differences that matter once we have engaged with them. This book not only prolongs this insight by depicting how teenagers' attachments form at small doses, thanks to specific spatial arrangements and caregivers' techniques, but it also hones this insight by showing that these spaces and techniques trigger *the smallest of them*. The idea of 'slightest attachment' was brought to my attention when I figured out that the team attempted to foster the teens' affinities at any possible degree. They tried to spark the smallest of attachments through the mediation of spaces. The superlative 'slightest', then, emphasizes that the existence of these attachments is fragile, tenuous, because these affinities depend on caregivers' acute ability to notice their instant emergence. For them, every little attachment manifests as an embryonic sketchy possibility, as a lesser being that demands a greater achievement of its existence (Lapoujade (2021 [2017]).[18] This idea will culminate in the fourth chapter. Attachments of quiet intensity, we then realize, even in their most minimal expression, provide a fertile ground to become of greater interest. They then bear important consequences for the care work, institutional life, and its place.

Sparking attachments as care work

There is another difference between sparking attachments in amateur practices and here, in care work. Whereas amateurs seek to produce their passion, the teenagers who come to the day center most often do not aim at seeking them out. But caregivers do. They attempt to lure

---

18   Lapoujade (2021 [2017]) explores this ontology of beings of 'lesser existence' in his perceptive essay about Souriau's work on the 'modes of existence'. In French, the expression "slightest" (moindre) also echoes two movies that feature an attentiveness to the sensorial experiences of patients (Philibert 1997) or of autistic children (Deligny, Manenti & Daniel 1962–1971). In these movies, such an attentiveness grants these inclinations a central importance in settings alternative to traditional psychiatric hospitals.

the teens' responses to things or activities that could possibly appeal to them.[19] From one person to another, and from one day to the next, their responses remained unpredictable. An adolescent might be inclined to engage with the lure, or they might firmly resist it. Both kinds of responses, whether manifesting an attachment or a detachment, led caregivers to adjust their reactions in turn. Of course, I rarely met teenagers who were constantly eager to take up whatever was suggested to them. And most of them expressed, at least at some point, ambivalent feelings about the care setting and what it expected of them. Although this seldom happened, I also met a few teens who were nearly always left cold by most activities or occurrences in the day center. These young people had typically gone through an unstable life path, such as having spent years in juvenile institutions. In the day center, their overly chaotic attitudes made it hard for them to stay longer than a few months. To say the least, although they represented a minority of the teens, it was puzzling to witness that these adolescents didn't seem to find an anchor anywhere.

The fact that the adolescents' affinities were of primary interest to the caregivers calls for two clarifications. First, a word on the issue of power. There was indeed a necessary power circulating in the various lures to teenagers, which – as far as I could observe – emanated from their peers, from the staff, or from the material arrangements. Yet this power should not be *a priori* understood as negative per se, as a mere domination technique that disciplined, prohibited or regulated. Enticement could also transform those who let themselves be 'turned on' to some preference or disinclination.[20] Insofar as this form of power reinvigorated personal

---

19   This luring process can be understood as a technique of influence that involves the mediation of spaces or objects. I will return to this point in more detail in the second chapter. For more on the practical operations of influence in psychotherapy inspired by non-Western healers, see Nathan (1994).

20   Gomart and Hennion (1999: 220) underline this characterization of power in the concept of attachment. They recall Foucault's warning about our understanding of power (1995 [1975]): "We must cease once and for all to describe the effects of power in negative terms: it 'excludes', it 'represses', it 'censors', it 'abstracts', it 'masks', it 'conceals'. In fact, power produces; it produces reality; it produces

affinities, it could empower people when those affinities came into being. Of course, a structural asymmetry was playing out between the team
and the teens. Yet when the spaces of the day center provided conditions
for the creation of attachments, these conditions offered possibilities for
teens to position themselves in practice, when developing relationships
to others and to things at hand in the course of daily care (Pols 2005;
2010). In these conditions, power was not just an evil that must be denounced. It was there, at stake, in the luring processes that I describe,
when teenagers and caregivers kept positioning themselves, negotiating, engaging, and resisting in their responses.

Second, an important theme that arose in this research was the
informal knowledge that working with attachments generates.[21] Indeed, when teenagers positioned themselves relationally, this enabled
the team to notice what moved them, and how each youth could have
changed, or not. This informal learning forms part of the 'situated
knowledge' that anthropologists have recognized in the psychiatric
teams who work in close contact with patients (Rhodes 1991: 173–174;
Floersch 2002; Brodwin 2013: 48–49). Such knowledge is homemade.
It takes shape alongside an accumulation of ordinary experiences, and
hence remains fragmentary, particular, local and hardly duplicable elsewhere. Above all, it is fragile when confronted with biomedical science.[22]
Here, the "informal" quality of this knowledge denotes that it is gained,

---

domains of objects and rituals of truth. The individual and the knowledge that
may be gained of him belong to this production." (Foucault 1995 [1975]: 194).

21   I further explore this informal knowledge in the second and third chapters.

22   This situated knowledge takes root in different understandings. Floersh invokes a common sense developed by caregivers. For Rhodes, the references are
Haraway (1988) and Foucault (1980). The latter speaks of "subjugated knowledge" to underline that it has "been disqualified as inadequate to their task or
insufficiently elaborated: naive knowledges, located low down on the hierarchy, beneath the required level of cognition or scientificity.", and that "[...] it is
through the reappearance of this knowledge, of these local popular knowledges, these disqualified knowledges, that criticism performs its work." (Foucault
1980: 82).

shared, and used in casual situations which necessarily involve inter-personal relations and engagements. When caregivers discussed teens' attachments, the informal knowledge base they created supported them in responding to each youth according to their inclinations or interests. This is what I call a "responsive" care practice: a practice in which care engages the teens, their caregivers, and their material mediations in a subtle play of personal and relational responses.

An enduring tension

The argument of this book – that spatial arrangements contribute to care as they generate a range of attachments, including the smallest of them – holds implications for contemporary conversations about psychiatric settings and, by extension, about institutional care. The issue that captures my concern is whether certain buildings and interior spaces hold potential to make room for the patients' personal responses, with their specificities, their struggles and their abilities. As the story of the day center indicates, the room made for biomedicine remains in tension with the sociotherapeutic work that considers patients as relational persons. In fact, this tension between the biomedical and so-cial conceptions of mental illness and therapy has traversed psychiatry buildings for ages. While entire bookcases would be necessary to trace it along that history up till today, I would like to take a shortcut with the purpose of introducing how the present study addresses this tension and intervenes in the current context of the psychiatric field.

This leads us to take a brief historical detour. In the 19th century, psychiatrists and architects collaborated to design asylums for what was called 'moral treatment' (Markus 1993: 133; Quétel 2010: 74). Back then, they conceived the spaces through the lens of "environmental determin-ism" (Yanni 2007: 8). The idea that the architectural environment could shape behavior was pushed forward, with the suggestion that it would also cure diseases. Concretely, this meant the removal of patients from their everyday environment; the internal organizations of buildings based on classification systems, like galleries and cells organized in rows; or hierarchical divisions of labor. In Europe, models of asylum spread as states mandated commissions to visit their buildings and to bring back their principles (Laget 2008). Since the early 20th century, though, a significant turn occurred as psychiatrists and architects started to lose their optimism. Asylums with their carefully determined arrangements did not prove to be a great remedy. On the contrary, the overcrowded services, in poor repair, with their meaningless routines, led to more damage than rehabilitation. Movements of "social psychiatry" started to envision care outside asylums, turning attention to the social condition of patients outside their walls (Lie and Green 2021). From the 1950s, antipsychotic medications started to be widely marketed and facilitated discharge of patients into their communities. Meanwhile, deterministic environmental convictions vanished, and architects' interest in conceptualizing care buildings dissipated (Yanni 2006; 2007: 145–158).[23]

From the mid-20th century, critiques increasingly shook the psychiatric field. They denounced, among others, its power relationships, institutional confinement, and the medicalization of mental illness. Several studies famously nourished these debates by drawing attention to spatial organizations. Foucault (1995 [1975]), in his historical analysis of disciplinary techniques, decorticated how the spatial partitions in institutions worked as power mechanisms. Buildings contributed to controlling docile bodies and transforming individuals' behavior while also making them observable for knowledge. His study became indispensable in the contestation of disciplinary architecture, for these spaces worked with a power mechanism and knowledge regime that dissolved the need for apparent corporeal violence (such as with chains). In 1961, Goffman foregrounded other issues in an ethnographic monograph of what he termed a "total institution" (4), a setting that fully takes

---

23   Perhaps it is less surprising, then, that historical research on the spatial conditions of psychiatry mostly focuses on the asylum era (in North America and Europe) and much less on its subsequent epoch of community care. See, for instance, Yanni (2007); Topp, Moran & Andrews (2007); Hamlett (2015); Ankele & Majerus (2020).

charge of the needs of inmates. Life within the psychiatric hospital, his study showed, led patients to experience a mortification of the self. While being isolated from the outside world, the inmates learned to see themselves through a ward system and had too few opportunities to build their personal territory within the institution walls.[24] This is how inmates, Goffman wrote, go through a dispossession from their personalities and from their ability to act in everyday situations. The book grew widely popular. It had a significant impact in anti-psychiatry movements, as well as on the public reforms that spread in many countries at that time.

In the wake of those critiques, among many others, psychiatric institutions underwent a thorough spatial reconfiguration. Deinstitutionalization policies aimed at moving away from long-stay psychiatric hospitals and promoted community-based facilities. Asylums were abandoned, hospital settings were reduced to acute care units and connected to a variety of new centers that were implemented within communities.[25] In contrast with traditional disciplinary architecture, these centers were often established in existing, small-scale buildings. They were entwined into neighborhoods and located at reachable distances by public infrastructure. From the outside, they were not clearly demarcated from other houses of the street. And their interior arrangements were often domestic while few, if any, of their features bore similarity to hospital institutions. Rather, as with the case we follow in this book, the arrangement of these houses wasn't rationally predetermined. The idea was that they remain flexible as to adapt to the possible upcoming uses of the particular people, including the patients, who frequented them (Baillon 1982).

---

24   Despite the "underlife" of the institution, in which patients resist what is expected from them in an attempt to regain a sense of their selves (Goffman 1961: 171–320).

25   These moves from hospital to the community did not occur in a similar way across countries and regions. A review of the literature here cannot do justice to that diversity. Gijswijt-Hofstra et al. (2005) give an insight of those local developments.

But in the following decades, the face of deinstitutionalization changed along the way. Starting in the 1950s with the ideal of freeing patients from wards, it turned into reduction of costs through the implementation of less expensive settings, under the label of managed care or of mobile teams.[26] Managed care developed in the United States to reduce hospitalization and support individuals' recovery at home, as well as other 'needs' of 'clients', supposedly by coordinating community-based services. While case managers tinker with an individual knowledge of their clients, these frontline clinicians largely work under the predominance of bio-psychiatry (Floersh 2002; Brodwin 2013). Meanwhile, like most psychodynamic practices that need time, availability, and money, many settings like therapeutic communities have been driven out of psychiatry. In Belgium, where my fieldwork is, today's public policies largely favor the establishment of ambulatory care, in which patients are visited in their own living environment by mobile teams, not only in prevention of crisis but for long-term support as well.

Holding room for personal responses

In this shifting context, the vision of what the care landscape becomes seriously undermines institutional spaces where patients could be hosted as relational persons (Estroff 1981: 254).[27] Institutional reform

26   The failure of the deinstitutionalization reforms is well documented. It has often resulted in abandoning people living with mental troubles in the street. Knowles (2000) shows this in an ethnography of the spaces occupied by people who are neglected by the community mental health system in Montreal.

27   In Belgium this mental health reform began in 2010. A recent study has investigated how this reform has been working so far in Brussels (Walker, Nicaise & Thunus 2019). The authors note that, according to care professionals, too much means are devoted to mobile teams compared to other kinds of facility. More importantly for my argument, this study brings out that many people with psychiatric troubles do find greater support in "places of connection" (*lieux de lien*), where the medical discourse is not predominant, if not altogether absent, since these places rather belong to the cultural or associative sectors. This finding confirms how much the actual places of encounters and where personal

entails another materialization of space: there are fewer or no longer any buildings where caregivers and peers meet daily, albeit not without friction, and slowly grow into a better state thanks to the specific relationships and appreciations they weave *there*. In other words, the emplaced therapeutic techniques that were developed as alternatives to hospitalization for half a century are now devalued, if not suppressed, in the name of cost reduction and management discourses promoting efficacy. These discourses rely on the scientism of neuro- or bio-psychiatry, or on rehabilitation programs based on a classification of mental disorders (Demailly 2011; Bellahsen & Knaebel 2020). This book responds to this corrosive situation by leaving no doubt about the crucial role of institutional buildings in community psychiatry, while their consideration seems all too often absent when envisioning the facilities of today and tomorrow.

But there is yet something more at stake in the erosion of spaces for community care and the devaluation of psychodynamic approaches in favor of biomedical ones. Lurhmann (2000), in her ethnography of psychiatrist training, points out that each approach implies a different way of conceiving mental trouble, of seeing patients, and of working with them. The loss of psychotherapeutic techniques, then, affects the way mental illness is conceived, narrowing it to be seen only as a disease, which impoverishes "our sense of human possibilities" (266). Such a disappearance entails the loss of close relationships with patients, loss of a deeper understanding of them, as well as loss of the complicated struggles and circumstances of each person. Above all, it implies the loss, within a care setting, of being able to provide *patients the possibility of responding* according to their unique, relational experiences.

Moreover, the problem is that in psychiatry and institutional care, the question of who or what a 'person' is cannot be easily solved. Along

---

affinities can anchor remain indispensable for care provision with the psychiatric landscape. A mobile team for young people in Brussels (Carton et al. 2020) makes a similar point. In their account of a youth's 'revolving door' trajectory (a succession of hospitalizations and discharges), they emphasize the great confusion that this discontinuous care causes for the youngster.

with Goffman's conclusion I mentioned above, medical anthropologists have brought to the fore how patients, once diagnosed with mental illness, see their status as person diminished, because they fail to act as unified and coherent centers of consciousness and of moral responsibility. These pathological diagnoses are formulated in ways that create a sense of the degradation of those capacities (Barham & Hayward 1991; Barrett 1996; Martin 2007).[28] The question of personhood in psychiatry remains quite tricky, insofar as it relies upon that conception of a 'person' with which patients have failed to align. In contrast, as we will see later, sociotherapeutic techniques and their spatial arrangements call for another conception of personhood. Here, it takes shape through a web of strong, intimate, reciprocal connections with others and with things that are crucial for restoring patients' personal and relational agency in the recovery journey (Troisoeufs 2009; Myers 2015).[29] The responses from teens that caregivers sought to provoke were not leashed to a conception of a person as an autonomous and rational individual. Quite the contrary, these community spaces and practice encouraged what a person

---

28   Martin (2007) writes that this Western conception of the person comes from the 17th century. It then included adult men, the 'men of reason'. During this period the 'mad' joined others who also did not possess full personhood, namely women, children, servants, and slaves. This is reminiscent of Foucault's (2001 [1961]) historical study that shows how madness was negatively defined as an absence of the work of reason. In her conclusion, Martin (2007: 277–280) takes up Foucault's argument: she states that this division is still at play nowadays, even though her descriptions of the experiences of people diagnosed as bipolar refute it. In the field of psychiatry, too, author-practitioners from distinct traditions narrate, and advocate for, patients who come to engage in a therapeutic work and in ways of living with their specific forces and abilities, instead of being defined as people with deficiencies. See Nathan (2001); Sacks (2012 [1995]); or Rogers (2020 [1967]) who inspired person-centered care frameworks in nursing studies.

29   In her ethnography of mental health care, Myers (2015) emphasizes the concept of 'moral agency' as it "suggests that in order for people to become the kind of person they want to be in the world, they must act in a way that helps others recognize them as the person they hope to be and holds them accountable for it" (156).

may be through the flourishing of their attachments, in much more livable ways.

In short, the disappearance of community work from the psychiatric
landscape entails the loss of possibilities for patients to be able to respond as particular people, in particular relationships, building upon
their specific affinities and their abilities to act with and upon the world
at hand, rather than solely (or alongside) coping with a disease and its
deficiencies. This tension has been at stake in psychiatric spaces since
their establishment and throughout the history of their contestation.
This book does not celebrate with nostalgia the heydays of social psychiatry or its therapeutic revolution. Nor does it provide an overview
of, or comparison between, the facilities that compose the psychiatric
landscape. Nor does it engage with the trajectories of patients in that
landscape, their struggles, or their lived experience of treatment.[30] But
it takes a partial perspective in order to revalue, among the different approaches that compose psychiatric and institutional care today, the community practice and its spatial mediations that still entertain the possibilities of both personal and collective responses in these places.

From fieldwork to a book

Between June 2013 and September 2015, I was intermittently immersed
in the care center before, during, and after the transition between
buildings. I began to take part in the care practice as most trainees do.
Besides that, I documented my experience with lots of note taking,
sketches, photographs, and recordings. During periods of two weeks
to several months, I spent whole days at the center, attending informal

---

30   Velpry (2008) provides such an account of patients' trajectory and everyday life
in France, Barham and Hayward (1991) in the UK, and Estroff's (1981) ethnography in the US remains a classic. Jenkins and Csordas (2020), inspired by pheno-
menological anthropology, have done such a study on adolescents' experience
of psychiatry. They conclude that the possibility of "having a life" (207) is cru-
cially at stake for those teens (ibid: 207–241). This resonates with the teens'
attachments that I describe in this book.

moments, workshops, and team meetings. I progressively learned to adjust my responses in everyday interactions. I conducted 45 private interviews with caregivers of each function and with teens, starting with three questions: what they usually do with the surrounding spaces, what changes in that materiality they had noticed, and what comparisons do they make with other institutional places where they had been. Most caregivers and teenagers had experienced other settings in hospitals or welfare facilities. When the design of the new building was still in the conception phase, I also respectively met the architects, administrative directors, or former caregivers of this institution, to better understand the context and stakes of that project.

My ethnographic method took a peculiar, unexpected turn when the move was approaching. Some caregivers saw my presence among them and the observations I had collected so far as an occasion to collectively address the matters of space that then started to worry them and the adolescents. They proposed that I would accompany the transition. I thereupon attended caregivers' meetings with architects. I joined visits of the building site with small groups of caregivers and teenagers. I held a workshop with teens reporting on the relocation from the old house to the new building. And I partook in debates about spatial problems, which kept arising until the second year after their move. Along the installation phase, we also organized several staff meetings, for the team to react to my observations while also discussing choices for settling into the new building. During these meetings, we could figure out which rooms and issues had already gained a smooth consensus within the team or with the architects, or which arrangements caused debate to erupt, the values embedded in them, and the material details that counted for them. In short, when fieldwork turned into a companionship of the transition, the research topic of this book – the material spaces in a care practice – evolved together with my interlocutors' relationship to it as a practical problem.

Accordingly, the translation of that field experience into a book pursues a distinct analytic path. Each chapter starts with a spatial problem that rose in the everyday practice or with the transition to the new building. Each problem draws attention to words that I selected since they mattered to caregivers in regard to the spaces, such as 'familiar', 'involve-ment', 'interest', or 'lively'. The teens sometimes seized on these terms too, for they pervaded the verbal world of the therapeutic community. However, they did not speak 'about' these words as concepts. Rather, the words point to values which played out in their interactions with the ma-terial spaces, creating opportunities to explore what these relationships entailed. My intention is to give more importance and nuance to these concepts by articulating my empirical descriptions and literature.[31] This analysis has led me to foreground the attachments of quiet intensity that now pervade this book.

In their everyday work, though, the team didn't explicitly speak with or about the term 'attachment' in the sociological sense, nor in a psychological sense. They did not refer to theories of attachment as formulated in the field of psychology and psychoanalysis, by Winnicott (1965) and Bowlby (1999 [1969]), among others.[32] However, caregivers' exchanges were dotted with words that pointed to the ways in which teens develop affinities, such as 'familiar', 'involve', or 'interest'. I came to understand these concepts as different forms of attachments that are brought into being by mediation of the spaces.[33] When I returned this

---

31   This does not mean depicting scenes as realistically as possible, but instead re-articulating the field experience, including the silent one, into written descrip-tions and insights. See Hirschauer (2006); Emerson, Fretz & Shaw (2011 [1995]).

32   This is another understanding of the notion of 'attachment'. It does not desi-gnate how appreciations come into being in socio-material worlds, but assu-mes that an individual's social and emotional development is enabled by the secure base provided through another's constant caregiving.

33   This is not to say that distinctive forms of attachment, like familiarity or invol-vement, are *ipso facto* bound to particular spaces. Rather my analysis refines the links between specific spatial arrangements and ways of attaching. This allows us to understand in detail how the former encourages the latter, and to further recognize these spatial subtleties elsewhere. For instance, as you will read the second chapter, you will learn that corners in the living spaces contribute to fa-miliarization by suggesting the adjustment of one's comfortable distance. This enables us to recognize, in the third chapter, that corners in workshops suggest such distance adjustments too. In this second case, they also attempt to better involve participants in the activity at hand.

proposition to the team, they found it of keen interest. They emphasized that, although the quest for the teens' affinities was somehow diluted as commonplace in their everyday work, it was constantly at stake. Indeed, they added, their spaces played a crucial role in that dynamic.

What comes next

In the following chapter, I explore a first form of slight attachment with the living spaces where, most of the time, everybody stayed or passed by in a sort of casual, informal closeness. Such familiarity provided caregivers with an informal knowledge of each teenager, thanks to which they adjusted the care work to their personal and changing nuances. The chapter unravels three different ways that the living spaces fostered or hindered familiarization. Certain things, like games, kindled the clustering of adolescents and caregivers around hotspots. Other arrangements enabled them to adjust the contact between them, like everyday objects whose use implied indirectly addressing one another; sight lines that invited discreet glances across rooms; or corners that offered a chance to finding one's right distance from others. And familiarity was also enacted while 'hanging out' with furniture that afforded informal postures, or with a semi-open kitchen and its cook that mediated informal encounters. The living spaces encouraged familiarization through these 'material suggestions'. In contrast with clearly functional places, these material suggestions are ambiguous 'affordances' (Gibson 1966) that allow contingent influences. They ease the discomfort of institutional pressure on teens, and frame familiarity as an opportunistic, or circumstantial, form of attachment.

We will then travel to different locations inside and outside the building, where caregivers and teens engaged in workshops. 'Involvement' is a keyword throughout the third chapter. I explore the conditions under which material spaces can involve the teens in activities. By noticing these involvements, the caretakers expand their informal knowledge. They can better see what a young person likes to do, what their sensibilities are, and the accompanying enthusiasms and difficulties. The adolescents' involvement in workshops is a highly uncertain form of attachment, for it happens between participants and things and requires specific practical and material framings. Through the setting of a pedagogical workshop that rejects the traditional classroom model, we learn how a space may arouse curiosity and allow caregivers to attune to teenagers' unsteady involvement in learning tasks. Meanwhile, the specific world of a clay workshop appeals to bodily senses and helps rekindle teens' engagement in modeling forms. Outings to sport fields and the city were porous to 'side slippage': unexpected disturbances that triggered collapse of the activity. But outside conditions also facilitated conversations. Beyond the contrasts between these different activities, these stories led me to see that workshop spaces, together with caregivers' techniques, facilitated teenagers' passage from indifference to greater involvement in what they were asked to do. Teen involvement, these passages show, is a form of attachment that comes into existence while remaining on the verge of fading.

When chapter four begins, almost a year had passed in the field. Material spaces varied over time as adolescents' and caregivers' interest in workshops declined and reawakened. Week after week, month after month, daily life activities carried a risk of boredom, and so required variation. New activities were set up, and the space was rearranged, evolving in response to the remaking of the teens' attachments. But how did all this happen? The chapter traces several strategies aiming at enrolling one another in interests current to the group. Such strategies became discernible in the hybrid arrangements of the buildings; in caregivers' exchanges about intriguing daily events; in their discussions with teens during community meetings – sometimes encountering their resistance; or in the adjustments of workshop frameworks alongside their realization. What's more, the interest and the spaces varied in less formal and verbal manners, along what we came to call 'waves'. As a workshop about bodily appearance exposed, this word evokes how participants' interest reshaped when taste for an activity spread within the group through interpersonal alterations. This chapter leads us to a turning point in the book. It brings into view that sustaining interest often relies on slight, furtive forms of attachment, such as the familiarity of the teens or their involvement in the moment. The slightest of these attachments nourished the care work, for the team understood every little teen affinity as an emerging possibility that could engage them in care and in their own trajectories. It turned out, too, that sustaining interest increased the importance of these modest affinities to the point of materializing them in the institutional spaces, keeping this place specific to what currently mattered within the group.

A clash in a staff meeting opens the fifth chapter. The argument erupted as caregivers discussed that the aesthetic style of the new building should impart it with 'something lively'. Among different traits of the material environment, the exhibition of teenagers' artworks was especially at stake for conveying this liveliness. The guides in this chapter are thus drawings, paintings, frames, posters, mosaic tiles, and other artworks waiting to be thrown away. Some of these things emerged from workshops, and these anecdotes enliven them with concerns for those who are still aware of those special moments. Artworks could also incite group members to tell stories. These narratives expand the present time to past moments and keep track of teens' attachments. A chalkboard, meanwhile, sees tensions emerge as it appeals to brief, casual involvements in writing inscriptions. The stories about these artworks train our attention to the temporalities that they carry. These stories foreground how much the liveliness of the building rests on the artworks' temporal overlaps. They prompt me to expand the argument that attachment formation is bound to specific temporalities. From the slightest affinity to larger interests, each of them requires unpredictable paces to come into being. These paces can hardly be foreseen on a smooth, linear timeline, and even less in exhibitions organized with calendars. Hence, care work must operate with these different and overlapping temporalities.

The book ends by calling attention to the subtle character of crafting the attachments of teens. This subtlety relies on both caregivers' intuitive and contingent techniques, and on the material spaces that contribute to it. This notion of subtlety conveys some of the ethical implications that this responsive practice and its spaces carry in psychiatry and institutional care. My purpose is to point out what makes caregivers' practice and spaces vulnerable in the broader psychiatric landscape, while also offering an acute sense of the vital role they continue to play as an institutional form of care in the community.

Chapter 2
Familiarity with living spaces

When I arrived in the field, Baptiste, the coordinator, told me an intriguing story about a change that had just occurred. On Monday mornings, the teens and a few caregivers gathered for a 'speaking group', where each teenager was invited to discuss an issue of current importance to them. Neither a psychotherapeutic group, in which participants were expected to expose their own difficulties, nor a meeting dedicated to the resolution of conflicts, the speaking group had been implemented by caregivers a few years earlier as they observed how uneasy it was for the adolescents to relate to each other as a group of peers. Hence it became important to create a space for casual discussions, fed by the adolescents' concerns only, for them to better constitute a group identity with its own significances. Since then, the speaking group had had its ups and downs. But in recent months, it had become a mess. Discussions gave rise to lots of tensions. Participants had become far more irritable. They didn't trust the confidentiality within the group anymore, to such a point that exchanges had turned idle or jammed.

Until some teenagers proposed moving the speaking group to the living room. Originally, caregivers didn't want to do it there because they saw the living room as mostly the teens' space, and they didn't want to intrude in it. So far, the speaking group had taken place in a multipurpose room where they brought cushions and everyone sat in a circle. But, as some of the teens told me later, the living room appeared to them a better space for feeling at ease and connecting with each other. It was a material environment where they were used to engaging with the other people and surrounding objects in familiar ways. So, it made sense to them that such informal exchanges occur there. After a few tries, the caregivers recognized that this use of the living room actually improved the flow of conversation and broke down barriers. Obviously, the familiarity that helped unblocking the conversation was connected to certain material spaces and not to others. This familiarity wasn't only a concern for the caregivers, who at first did not want to intrude in the space, but also for the teenagers. They identified that their familiar bonds, having been anchored in the living room, were convenient for easing talk.

The concern about familiarity came up again with the subject of the move to the new building. Caregivers wished to maintain living spaces – a living room coupled with a kitchen and a yard – that created convivial feelings and warmth, that were welcoming and familiar. Among caregivers' terms to describe these qualities, 'familiarity' is the most accurate word to describe the making of personal acquaintances, informal attitudes, and closeness in relationships I experienced in the field. The development of familiar bonds with other members of the group and with the surrounding things was a form of light attachment that I understood as crucial for sociotherapy. And certain material traits of the living spaces fostered the making of such familiar webs, while others disabled it. So, I wondered, how do these living spaces contribute to the enactment of familiarity? And how is this way of attachment useful for care?

While framing familiarity as a practical achievement, in what follows I examine the institutional ambiguity of the living spaces as both domestic setting and workspace. This draws attention to the core role of familiar bonds in daily sociotherapy: it provides caregivers with an informal knowledge of each teenager, enabling them to adjust the care work to their personal and changing nuances. I then explore three ways in which daily interactions with these living spaces enable familiarity to occur (or not), when adolescents and caregivers cluster around hotspots, adjust the contact between each other, or hang around without much involvement in activities. I end by discussing how the affordances of the living spaces foster the creation of familiar bonds through 'material suggestions'. In contrast with clearly functional places, these material suggestions allow contingent influences, ease the institutional pressure on teens and, finally, frame familiarity as an opportunistic, or circumstantial, form of attachment.

Practicing familiarity

After hearing the story of the speaking group, it was by gleaning hints here and there that I progressively discerned how 'familiarity' was done in practice. I noticed how a familiarizing process passes from strangers' indifference to closer and more informal interactions and acquaintances. How would that happen in practice? Hirschauer (2005) provides an insightful study of 'strangeness' as a practical accomplishment. He describes the enactment of indifference with the spatial setting of an elevator. While the materiality of the narrow but still public space of an elevator lacks occupational opportunities, which therefore inhibits people's actions, the 'doing of nothing' flows through multiple tiny adjustments: automatic doors require precise timing for entering and exiting; the car's small size induces specific body placements with an awareness of distance-keeping and forces positioning in 'half-turns' towards others (51); and the proximity makes participants avoid eye contact, often preferring to turn their gaze to the floor. These descriptions indicate how much 'strangeness', the un-relatedness with insignificant others, is maintained through interactions with a material space. The elevator space provides few opportunities for other occupations besides finding face-to-face with other participants who devalue their copresence (ibid: 59).

Hence, establishing familiar bonds would not begin with an absence of interaction. Rather, it shifts from a complex way of enacting indifference towards doing the familiar, with a material environment providing opportunities for that shift.[1] Such a practical engagement is noticeable

---

1   Ethnographic studies about spatial arrangements as mediators of sociability have mainly focused on people's engagement and estrangement with each other in public spaces (Gieryn 2000: 476–477). Whyte (1980), for instance, in his empirical study of New York urban spaces, reports many arrangements that

in concrete interactions, in body positions, placements and distances, ways of looking (or avoiding looking), or in paying attention, facial expressions, the back-and-forth dynamic of responses to these engagements from the environment or other people, and their reenactments at an everyday pace.

But the personalized relationship I noticed with the living spaces deepened far beyond momentous interactions. Over time, along with personal accommodations to the environment, a teen's personality could be diffused by things, and be constituted through familiar bonds with these things. In this way, it was a form of attachment. This is an idea that Thévenot (1994; 2001) formulates in his analysis of the "familiar regime." A regime designates a practical mode of access to a tangible environment that in turn responds to someone's movements, and it implies an orientation towards certain kinds of goods rather than others. One regime Thévenot identifies is that of "conventional functionality" of things (2001: 70), or of planned actions, in which people's engagement with a nearby surrounding is based on regular use in accordance with functional design. We can, then, see the smooth elevator car and its buttons for controlling the doors or moving up and down as objects of conventional utility. In contrast, Thévenot writes, the familiar regime "rests on an accustomed dependency with a neighborhood of things and people" (ibid: 77). Here is how he casts this process:

> 'Intimate' familiarization evokes a direct corporal implication, the idea of a tight union between bodily gestures and an environment which makes for highly local convenience. The dynamics of the relationship between the human and nonhuman entities which compose familiar surroundings are highly dependent on personal and local clues that were made out as salient features for adjustment in the commerce for these familiar beings. In this regime, agents are guided by a wide range of sensorial clues, as well as indications from spatial positioning.

---

support sociability, such as sitting ledges that invite informal and relaxed bodily positions (28–33).

[...] Such clues are widely distributed in the web of connections which
sustain familiarity. (ibid: 70)

Such a web of familiar bonds with a surrounding constitutes an "attached personality" (ibid: 77), extends it, and maintains it in time.
Moreover, such personal uses have their own way of becoming collective. They cannot be directly shared with a newcomer, as would dictate
the regime of functional conventionality. Instead, the transmission of
personal uses must be learned through a process of accommodation to
another personality, by developing connections to its familiar world.
The practical achievement of familiarity, then, progressively leads to a
customized web of mundane attachments to the things and people that
are present.

In this chapter, I build on this pragmatic characterization of the
familiar to tackle the idea that a surrounding environment is not only
something caregivers and teenagers become accustomed to, but the
space also presents material traits for weaving familiar webs with things,
people, and the environment. Such material traits offer 'affordances'
(Gibson 1966) for familiarizing, meaning that their material features
one can perceive (size, shape, texture, color, positioning, motion, etc.)
furnish the observer who interacts with that materiality the experience
of (inter)personal accommodation. Before exploring in greater detail
how these affordances work, let me address the importance to the care
practice of weaving these familiar webs.

Workspaces for informal knowledge

The living spaces of the care home held an institutional ambiguity, since
they were at once the caregivers' workplace and a domestic layout for
sharing everyday moments with the teens. On the ground floor of the old
house, the living room was laid with an old parquet and offered a large
sofa in an angle and another, smaller one, both facing a blocked fireplace
and the two high bookcases that flanked it (figure 6). On the other side of
the narrow vestibule, the dining room was adjoined by a kitchen (figure

7). Both rooms overlooked a small courtyard surrounded by the trees and back houses of the neighborhood.

Such a domestic scene was not reminiscent of a disciplinary setting. Rather, it invited a much more chaotic web of interactions. It tended to blur everyone's roles, by not defining in advance the ways of relating, say as hosts, friends, or professionals. At first glance, we may think that such a domestic surrounding would foster the kinds of sociality one usually finds with family or in a private home.[2] But the familiarity I encountered with the living room, kitchen, dining room, yard, and vestibule of the day center did not give an evident sense of family relationships. What I experienced with teenagers and caregivers were other forms of closeness and acquaintance: it involved personal accommodations that blurred with professional ways of relating, although these did not remain given. As one teenager shared with me, newcomers joined the group every so often (mostly teens or trainees), so familiarity was propagated in particular by acting as a host or guest. Yet, I remember a caregiver telling me that it happened that they openly questioned the nature of their relationships with teens, without easily finding the right words. Familiar webs were both personal and professional, and both ways of relating remained partially undetermined.

Within the therapeutic community model, these unprescribed relationships allowed unexpected occurrences with teens in an everyday

---

2   It would be tempting to bind the process of familiarizing with the 'homely' aspect of these spaces. But it would go too fast. My interviews in the field challenged the assumption that familiarity relates, above all, to homely or familial environments. Teens who lived full time in residential institutions debunked this presumption with very different logics. Personalized landmarks, some declared, could be achieved in places that were not, or didn't feel, 'at home'. Etymologically, too, the definition of 'familiar' has always spanned beyond biological-family relationships; this form of acquaintance and intimacy with something or someone isn't especially bound to the sharing of a household (Oxford English Dictionary online, s.v. "Familiarity", accessed December 04, 2016). Wilkinson (2014) underlines this nuance with single people. See also Pasveer, Synnes and Moser (2019) for diverse accounts of the work involved in the making of 'home' in care for elderly people.

context, to which the sociotherapists responded. That is, from 9am to 5pm, when they shared meals, casual moments, and diverse activities, the caregivers did not "simply do" these things with teens, but they did it "with a particular listening to it, and with a particular response to it", as one of them explained to me. Too much familiarity, then, risked becoming a pitfall when a caregiver responded to an occurrence with mere spontaneity, losing awareness of "what was actually happening at a given moment" to respond in a slightly different way. In other words, while mundane events of ordinary life were crucial pivots, both on the spot and during debriefing meetings, familiarity so firmly embedded caregivers' professional role in interpersonal encounters that it might sometimes jeopardize the care work when it made caregivers lose sight of that role.

The domestic setting as a workspace, and the personal connections within professional ways of relating, were an important ambiguity for the care practice because it allowed the formation of an informal knowledge of the teens. Again Thévenot (1997), in his distinction between the familiar and the functional regimes, underlines how a workspace that incites familiar relationships also enables the production of informal knowledge. A clearly functional spatiality, in contrast, delimits each one's role and often relies on preconceived representations (or formal knowledge). Of course, the familiar and the planned regimes are often articulated empirically, but their distinction allows a better discernment of which mode of engagement might prevail in a practice and place.

This distinction between workplaces affording informal and formal knowledge is also identifiable in ethnographies of psychiatric settings. One of them takes place in a long-term mental health care setting. Pols (2005) discerns how silent patients enact appreciation in interactions with others and in a material environment that enables it. She tells the story of Dora, whose perspective becomes noticeable in her way of "practicing morning coffee": she does not join the conversation, but sits around a corner and knits, sometimes smiles about what has been said, and does the dishes when coffee time is over. In doing so, "she creates a situation with which she feels comfortable" (213). Nurses come to know what patients like and dislike through their personal accommodations when in such a situation. They try to learn about patients' perspectives as emerging positions in interactions, not as representations belonging to an individual. Becoming acquainted with patients in a same space and situation opens up more possibilities to deal with less asymmetrical relationships, instead of trying to conceal them, inasmuch as patients' appreciations can be taken into account only when trying to learn about them (ibid: 218). In contrast, Rhodes (1991: 11–33) depicts how the disciplinary space of an emergency psychiatric practice offers few occasions for seeing patients' perspectives and their nuances. The area at the back is a "holding environment", where "patients are soothed by such a place" and "motivated to leave it" (ibid: 33). The rooms provide them with no activities. Rather, that materiality witnesses their monotonous days. In the front part of the unit, the spatiality of the staff area structures different functions: the higher the status, the more mobile, private, and distant they are from patients. Rhodes analyzes the consequences of that spatial partition for the way caregivers see patients: as "wholly others" (ibid). This doesn't mean that the staff relied on scientific knowledge of medicine only. They also developed a particular and local knowledge of patients, "visible only from where they stood" (ibid: 174). But such knowledge wasn't favored by the spatial arrangements; if it was formed, this happened in the margins. Clearly these disciplinary spaces didn't afford their users the conditions for familiar and informal acquaintances.

The contrast between these two studies forges closer links between caregivers' workplaces and their informal knowledge of patients: while being in the same rooms and observing how they interact there, they can perceive how personal and changing nuances singularize each person. As teenagers became familiar with that environment, the team gained an informal knowledge of them. They collected small details when closely relating with the adolescents and noticed how each of them found their own way within the domestic layout. In interviews, the teenagers as much as the caregivers depicted their interactions with the living spaces according to things they liked to return to: beyond affinities or disfavor with others, they evoked material and sensory elements such as the smell of french fries, the comfort of a sofa due to its shape and fabric, whether the music player was on or off, the coffee thermos, the sun in that part of the yard, at that moment of the day, or a corner in the back, where they could escape the caregivers' gaze.[3] Alongside these mundane engagements, the familiarity each teen developed with the living spaces and the others in presence made more visible some of their personal inclinations in the flow of daily events.

How did this informal knowledge contribute to the care work? Caregivers frequently exchanged stories of this shared daily life during their meetings or chats in their office, so that this informal knowledge quickly grew for every staff member. Once they had created a portrait of a teenager, the caregivers were able to refine their attention and noticed smaller changes that had become surprising to them. Safia was a quiet adolescent who spent about two years in the center before she turned eighteen. For a long time, she stuck to her routines. She ate breakfast at the same table, often sat at the same seat on the sofa, and almost never spoke. She sometimes answered by nodding her head. She made very few movements, merely keeping her gaze facing ahead. Other teenagers teased her, but she rarely engaged in interactions. Until the day she started challenging the familiar portrait all had so far been acquainted with. Several caregivers reported greater bodily involvement in activities, or her amusement at silently contravening the seating conventions at a workshop. Tiny changes also became noticeable in the house, as when she agreed to play ping-pong, or when she encountered her own image in a mirror and did a small dance step to the side. As with many teenagers, their familiarity with Safia enabled the team to notice these minor changes, in contrast with her usual stillness. Without having sketched this intimate portrait day by day, those minor changes would most probably not have been surprising. These changes reshaped caregivers' informal knowledge. From there, they would respond differently to the youth.

---

3   One may rightly question this constant awareness of caregivers as a form of diluted surveillance, as a sort of panopticon that would have shifted from the building structure to the staff copresence. I rather came to see it as subtle, non-innocent technique that obliges the team to remain reflexive on it, like when they discussed how teens should access out-of-sight corners. I return to this issue at the end of the book.

At the same time, too much familiarity was a point of tension in the care practice that called for zones of negotiation. Although the center was a refuge where social norms were much suppler compared to teens' outside social life, the facility must also remain a transitional setting so that they could find ways to live beyond their stay. Yet too much relational ease could well turn familiar bonds into improper modes of conduct marked by undue freedom towards others. Caregivers had rules to prevent close contact from becoming too tense. But again, within everyday turbulence, strictly applying these rules was counterproductive for the caregivers' relational practice. The responses caregivers gave to Maxime shed light on this. This sporty young guy could not stop seeking trouble with others, as "he knew where to pinch them", a caregiver observed, in addition to his shouting, loud jumping on the stairs, and his attempt to start a fire. Obviously, his explosive state probably exceeded improper familiarity, and threatened the possible ease, informal contact, and closeness of others. Applying the rule would mean excluding Maxime from the center. But care work required working in a zone of negotiation where caregivers tried to understand what was happening for him. One morning, since they had noticed Maxime exploding each time he was back in the group, they proposed that one of them would spend time with him individually. Their informal knowledge of him colored their attempt to "contain him with the relationship", which was assessed together with an adjustment of his medication. The personal acquaintance created with Maxime supplied the care work with information even when his actions turned nasty. Familiarity did not only encompass comfortable ways of being together. Such attachment, because it opened a path for greater personal and relational ease, was always on the edge of becoming tricky. Caregivers adjusted their responses to the teenagers by creating zones of negotiation with them, thanks to the informal knowledge they gained in their relational closeness and acquaintance. Now, how did the spatial arrangements help to cultivate that familiarity?

Figure 6: The living room in the old house.

Figure 7: The dining room in the old house.

Clustering hotspots

From the first days of my fieldwork, it quickly became apparent how much the living spaces displayed objects, most of them games, inciting the improvisation of clusters of teens. These objects provided opportunities for assembly around 'hotspots': the spots where an action between several participants can begin, and grow more popular as they attract others to join in. Hotspots, I noticed, led to anchored personal landmarks in particular areas of the living spaces while teens engaged in informal encounters with the others involved. Hotspots were all but homogeneous, smooth encounters. They were at best fueled with an unstable atmosphere, full of ambiguous addressing, and shifting over time. At worst, they were deserted or blown up.

I first experienced a hotspot when taking part in a roleplaying game. This game was popular in the group at that time. When Gael, a caregiver, invited the teenagers to participate, in just a few minutes about ten participants were sitting on the sofas, facing each other, with the door of the living room shut to disturbances. The roleplay involved an adventure scenario where each of us hid an assigned character that the other players had to discover. Cards were dealt and drawn, questions were asked and answered in search of clues, looks of complicity or suspicion were given. While we had to find ways to feint with each other, the roleplaying game – as with all games that require guessing others' intentions and build suspense – brought layers of ambiguity into our interactions.[4] This cre-

---

4   Many scholars who study play have noted this ambiguity between a present situation and how participants understand it. Here I am interested in the potential of ludic devices for opening up divergent understandings of a situation, in relation to its salience in care institutions where relationships are asymmetrical and challenging. On this particular point, see Zaccaï-Reyners's (2015) reading of the notion of 'play' among different thinkers, in which she emphasizes the features of this notion that are helpful in care contexts. See also Haraway's conceptualization of "playing with strangers" (2007: 232; 232–246). In her multispecies account, play offers an experience of a joyful inventiveness where partners let go of the literal, logical, functional, and purposeful, and instead put at risk

ated a hotspot full of insinuation in the encounter. Tensions escalated, to such a point that a teenager suddenly dashed out of the room.

The instant the game ended, most of the teens rushed out the door too. "It often ends like that", Gael sighed to me. The game involved ambiguities within closeness. This combination easily provoked strong, impulsive, and sometimes violent responses. Although there were also short moments where the contact was easier, I could feel how the balance between ease and tension in the group was unstable. Participants often reacted to this instability by adjusting their bodily distance, whether being actively involved with the game, paying attention to what was happening, or retreating their bodies a bit from the scene. The broad seats of sofas allowed such bodily adjustments, as I noticed with a thin, very pale girl next to me who, without playing or saying a word, regularly retreated to the end of the sofa. It seemed that while the group dynamic was fragile and might easily get out of control, hotspot attendants were *spacing*. Goffman (1963) describes spacing as a way of making a space with bodies through the handling of distances and of orientations within interactions, which also ensures lines of speaking and exchanging of glances (161). Here, the spacing of participants was a way to facilitate closer contact while dealing with the tight and unstable strain of a hotspot. While the shut door limited the distance of these adjustments, the sofas with broad seats surrounding the living room enabled these discreet repositionings.

Hotspots were also mobile as their popularity fluctuated over time. During the first ten days of my fieldwork, most interactions occurred around sofas in the living room, on benches in the yard, at the ping-pong table, or with two other popular games. At the time, it often happened that the sound of ping-pong balls and the players' movement raised the attention of people nearby and drew them closer, which activated these areas as hotspots. Then the group composition varied, and hotspots moved. Once teens grew acquainted with each other, they might turn their interest to other areas. Another corner, table, bench, game, or

---

whether one's understanding is meaningful to the other partner in face-to-face interactions.

thing stole the limelight. As weeks passed, varying relationships among the group moved these transient clusters and provisionally enlivened hotspots. Following this inconstancy, the familiar bonds created with these clustering objects remained fluid.

From my first days at the care center, hotspots were the best places to become familiar with something, some area, or someone. Temporarily popular objects presented opportunities for participants to cluster informally. In doing so, they particularized their interpersonal and local conveniences in the living spaces. Hotspots would not liven up without the cluster-inducing objects scattered here and there. So, the objects and the hotspots they animated were key elements for the mundane and familiarizing encounters they enabled. Plus, due to the greater closeness hotspots entailed, and sometimes even ambiguities (as with games) and tensions, they spurred participants to enact spacing to better deal with their tight instability. These adjustments of bodily positions seemed necessary in the familiarizing process. As time passed, the mobile hotspots recorded and inscribed the dynamic way in which familiarity resettled unpredictably over time, as the group and relationships varied, without getting stuck into monotonous routine.

Contact adjustments

In just a week, it was easy to be acquainted with the collective use of the objects, their placements and displacements through the day, or the approximate hour the coffee thermos was most probably empty. I soon learned about Asma, the girl who had stayed silent and retreated during the roleplaying game. During the days following the game, my contact with her went easily. But creating familiar bonds with the surroundings and other people wasn't always so smooth. The weaving of early, unsteady, and friable affinities with others could well require some contact adjustments. In the three following ways, the material arrangements of the living spaces allowed for such adjustments.

Contact adjustments first occurred when caregivers or teens were casually addressing someone else. This was best achieved if the addresser was at the crossroad of different interactions. A plethora of things that were accessible to all in the living spaces enabled those concomitant interactions, and hence the addressing of one another in indirect ways. The morning I met Emile, about ten of us were busy preparing lunch in the cooking workshop in the dining room. Emile, a sturdy and outspoken teenager, sat at a table, his head resting on his crossed arms, hinting at a sullen mood. He felt too tired to engage, he said, but he didn't withdraw to rest either. Earlier that morning, on the way to the grocery store, we had spoken a bit about Bulgaria, his native country, which I had visited many times. As I passed by the table where he sat, I asked him another question about his country. But, as I had observed other caregivers doing, I didn't ask it straight forward. I chose my moment while passing by him on the way to the trash can, with some potato peels I had just picked up. This was a way of adjusting the contact to make it less formal. It was easier to refer to our previous chat while being in the middle of doing other things, where attention was being given to other objects, people, or activities surrounding us. Asking him in this manner made it just a casual question among many other engagements. It was a lighter inducement, for it was less directly addressed to him. If I had sat down opposite him and asked head-on, Emile would most likely not even have raised an eyebrow. Instead, his answer to my question turned into a chat, and drew both of us back to Bulgarian landscapes. He suddenly stood up, moved toward the sideboard and, handing me a few plates, asked if I would set the tables with him.[5] So we did. Setting the table made sense after I had cleared them of food waste, and the tableware was waiting right there, in the dresser nearby. That Emile offered to do it together could well have

---

5   Here Emile's response didn't solely concern the making of familiarity with him and the spaces, but also his involvement in an activity, the cooking workshop. This is another form of attachment that I explore in the next chapter. The casual way of addressing someone, who will then involve themselves in an activity, is a technique that closely echoes what Driessen (2018) coins, in another care context, as "sociomaterial will-work" (115). With this expression she describes the strategies of caregivers who try to sculpt the will of residents with dementia who really don't want something. The will-work she observes also relies on the materiality caregivers tinker with.

been a way of pursuing the interaction by other means than a face-to-face conversation. The conversation with Emile was also made informal thanks to concomitant interactions, thanks to the range of objects that were both available and opportune in an ongoing situation. With those everyday objects, making and resuming contact relied on very informal adjustments, whether one was just asking a question or offering to set the tables.

Later that day, contact adjustments with Emile occurred again, this time through discreet glances. It happened as I came down to the living room. One youth was reading, another playing a game with a caregiver. At the moment I came in, a third stood up and went to the dining room to grab a coffee. So I took his seat on the sofa. From there, I saw the dining room through the door and vestibule, and the yard through the dining room window. It was then that I glimpsed Emile who was outside, smoking a cigarette. He sat on the edge of the window and looked inside. Our eyes met. For a few seconds, our gazes locked. Then he turned his head to take a puff, and my attention came back to the living room. I then came to notice that glimpses of each other offered another sort of contact adjustment. They occurred in several articulated rooms whose layouts afforded such brief eye contact. At the day center, one could see from different angles through the various rooms that comprised the living spaces. Open doors, windows, wall openings and nooks standing between our gazes sharpened sightlines and prevented one from visually scanning the entire space (figure 8). From the sofa, I could be close to others sitting nearby, but for a very short moment I could also discreetly resume contact with Emile who was outside. Interactions lay in the discreet perceptions we may have had of each other, when resuming contact in highly informal ways, thanks to sharp sightlines between the different living rooms.

The third way to adjust my contact with others, next to casual addressing and discreet glances, surfaced thanks to a spatial problem. Since the living spaces of the old townhouse were small and confining, the teens felt too cramped, and they grew highly agitated. Lacking the right distance, interactions were prone to become more impulsive and offensive. A greater distance was needed for the teenagers to feel on their own while remaining part of the group, without tensions running too high. In other words, too much proximity obstructed the development of personal accommodations and closer relationships, which could then be eased by the negotiation of one's presence with others.

It must be said, one of the main reasons the caregivers wanted to move to a different place was the need for a sufficient number of square meters. In the new building, the living spaces were much bigger. However, though more space could help to ease tensions, caregivers discussed with the architects two design strategies that would fine-tune the problem of finding one's own distance in everyday practice. Whereas the caregivers' concern was prompted by their experience of tensions among teens, the architects referred to Hall's famous study (1966) about the conditions for intimate, personal, social or public distancing.

Both caregivers and architects first reckoned that the articulation of several different rooms would allow adjusting one's right distance. Thus, they reproduced in the new building a spatial configuration similar to the old house: the living room, dining room, kitchen, and courtyard/garden were separated but still near each other. All could be closed off from the others for occasional activities, but most of the time the doors remained wide open. While an ensemble of open rooms was a key feature to allow moving from one to another, each room's respective purpose suggested the shifting from one to another. Rather than a vast plateau of open space, the separation of respective rooms did not only afford discreet glances; it also suggested an informal circulation of people. Finding one's own ideal distance from others also came along through that circulation.

The second strategy was to implement corners for withdrawing into the design of the new living spaces. The architects sought to arrange corners that were neither too closed off nor too remote. For the living room, they used sofas to create one main sitting area and another smaller one, which was a bit apart from the rest of the space in a nook (figure 9). And they arranged more withdrawal nooks with smaller, reception sofas in parts of corridors that were broadened. These corners for withdrawing, in the living room and nearby areas, were meant to suggest that teens and caregivers could leave overcrowded spots and find space and quiet.

In doing so, the caregivers hoped they would suggest the distance adjustments that were crucial for creating familiar bonds and eluding tension.

Once in use, the articulation of rooms and corners for withdrawing proved to be design strategies that worked quite well to better deploy the occupants' mundane choreographies. Several teens reported that a few weeks of being in the new living spaces had helped to ease tensions a lot, and most of the time, circulation remained lively. Sometimes, though, the staff noticed the reverse effect: the living spaces now also risked becoming too quiet, meaning there was not enough movement. But overall, these arrangements clearly allowed the familiarization of each person with others and the place through distance adjustments.

Distance adjustments differed from the repositioning of bodies towards others of 'spacing'. Instead, they were comprised of the very mundane circulation of one's footsteps, preferring to go here or there throughout the day. While the design strategies subtly encouraged such distance adjustments in the care practice, they contributed to each person's negotiation of presence within their surroundings, according to what was happening from one moment to another. In interviews, several teens stressed that the improvised paces of these distance adjustments were a key difference from disciplinary settings, mostly schools or psychiatric wards, where spaces and moments of circulation were clearly delineated. As one teen, Karina, emphasized, the conditions for circulation in the day center were flexible: instead of the long corridors of hospitals or schools where one must walk some distance to reach a spot, here you could switch from one room to another in the space of a moment.[6] Caregivers, too, adjusted their distance through these

---

6   Karina's point could not have been more right. Corridors are key to the large-scale institutions that have been established since the 19th century, including the asylums of moral treatment, where they distributed and classified individuals, and prevented spontaneous mingling among them (Luckhurst 2019: 157–210). In Goffman's 'total institution' (1961, cited in Luckhurst 2019), though, some of its hallways constitute 'refuges' for the inmates' 'underlives' that the professionals tolerate.

ordinary placements and displacements when they attempted to generate the 'right atmosphere'. Noise often guided their game of presence and absence, by inciting them to come cheer up a room that had fallen silent, or to straighten teens out if they overheard some boisterous activity.[7] The mere unexpected distribution of attendants gave hints for adjustments, as Rachid, a nurse, put it:

> Yesterday, for instance, I wanted to settle in the living room. But then I saw that some trainees were already there. Each was busy speaking with a youth. So I didn't go, because I didn't want to overload the presence.

To negotiate one's own degree of presence among others was part of the care work, for those providing and receiving it, while engaging them in a familiarizing process.[8] As Baptiste explained in the story of the speaking group that opened this chapter, despite caregivers' precedence over teens in ordering the place, the former also wanted the living spaces to belong to the latter, thus letting them find their own familiar landmarks there. The articulation of rooms and corners for withdrawing that suggest distance adjustment, then, worked with that territorial ambiguity of the living spaces. These material arrangements drew teens and care-

---

7   Distance adjustments are often entwined with the calibration of the sound ambiance. Such adjustments are done thanks to a diffuse way of listening that I called "to lend an ear": when one let their attention be caught by surrounding noises or stillness. See d'Hoop (2020).

8   The suppleness with which a care receiver negotiates degrees of privacy is a pivotal dimension of many care situations. Twigg (1999) discusses the spatial ambiguity of privacy in care in the case of the provision of bathing in the people's own homes. There, caregivers manage this ambiguity by reordering (or not) boundaries between more private or public areas of the house. More broadly, it's worth noting that today's ordinary search for privacy in a house became the substratum of domestic architecture in the modern era in Europe. It was achieved thanks to spatial strategies, like limiting the number of doors in a room, or channelling circulation in passages like hallways and staircases. On the emergence of that sensibility together with its spatial configurations, see Evans (1997[1978]).

givers every day, or rather every moment, into mundane choreographies that blurred professional and personal ways of relating.

Figure 8: Map of the sightlines in the old house.

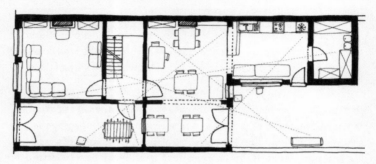

Hanging out

With the relocation to the new building, sofas became the subject of an interesting failure story. They were such ordinary things in the daily practice that nobody noticed how crucial they were, until they went missing. A few days after moving into the new space, the sofas had not yet been delivered. This provoked a crisis that was quite unexpected: without them, the teenagers quickly dispersed throughout the building, or simply left the day center. Caregivers were soon exasperated because they had, in their words, "to run after teens" to find them. This devastated the subtle play of movement between them that was necessary for their relational practice. Searching for the teens turned the informal relationship into a disciplinary one. They needed stronger 'anchor points' that everyone could pass by and where they could likely find others, without even really settling down. When the sofas finally arrived, the situation recovered its balance. Obviously, they were central to sustaining the group's loose but necessary cohesion. The absence of the sofas jeopardized the casual togetherness made possible by hanging out near anchor points in the living spaces.

The sofa crisis led me to look back at observations that were progressively invading my field-note journal, though they sounded trivial when I first jotted them down. They depicted scenes where nothing seemed to be happening, but where everyone was relating to each other and to the surroundings in a rather loose way. Like, someone grabs a coffee, while someone else moves from one game to observing another. Others settle down in one place, then join a chat elsewhere. Or someone goes to the kitchen to ask about the preparation of the meal. Why did I record these seemingly insignificant anecdotes? Reading them again, it became trenchant that the familiarity enacted with these living spaces took shape, too, when the teens hung out or lay around without seeming involved in what we were doing. The living spaces provided affordances for personal ways of relating that weren't firmly structured as in planned activities. How did they do that?

Back to the sofas. They were not only anchor points for hanging out or settling down. They were also objects for resting the body. The sofas were made of fabric, and together with cushions and footstools they allowed the body to relax, whether sitting, lying down, or finding a way between both postures.[9] The sofas were at angles or facing each other, as were the benches in the yard, or in the new building, a bar with stools in the kitchen that encouraged conversation among us. In a more improvisational way, leaning on your elbows on a working surface, on a low wall, or against a doorframe also allowed loose bodily positions during interactions. Our corporal engagements with these sitting and leaning elements set the tone of our chats, stories, thoughts, anecdotes, news, and jokes that we shared throughout the day. 'Hanging out' occurred through the relaxed bodily and speaking attitudes that most of us adopted in our

---

9   Sennett (1976) traces the advent of what was called, in the early 19th century, the 'comfortable': chairs, divans, and sofas, made of cushions for relaxing bodily postures between sitting and lying down (338–342). When mass manufacturing developed, these objects reached the wider public and invaded living rooms.

own way, in our interactions with sofas, benches, doorframes or counter-tops. Such informal interactions contradicted the more straightforward professional and educational relationships. Again, they contributed to blurring the differences between each person's role.

As I tried to understand how 'hanging out' worked, it was impos-sible not to notice a major aspect of the living spaces: the presence of the kitchen, with its specific layout and cook. Hanging out around the kitchen and the cook was a way of familiarizing that appeared especially welcome in regard to the danger of institutional routines. A typical day at the center was structured with breakfast, lunch, afternoon snacks, meet-ings, departures for activities, or returns from outings. I had been at the center for less than a week when I became aware of how much the repeti-tion of those daily activities threatened the care work to become incred-ibly dull for everyone, a least, if each day unfolded identically to the one before it. But that wasn't the case at all. Take lunchtime. It was a signif-icant gathering where all the teenagers ate with most of the caregivers. And it was scheduled at 12:30 each day. But we did not all arrive at the same time, serve, eat, nor clean up nor even leave together. We would hang around as the meal was being prepared as well as after we finishing eating. The dining room and kitchen became crowded at varying paces. As we bumped into each other when making our way through the space, seemingly casual proposals could be made, such as invitations to sit at a table, and dodges of these interactions as well. Towards the end, the group would progressively fade, with some staying to wash the dishes.

Hanging out in the kitchen before, during, and after lunch emerged as the most persistent hotspot. Over time, the kitchen and the cook remained a luring point that mediated indirect encounters between teens and caregivers. How was that accomplished? The transition to the new building emphasized the importance of the details of the kitchen's material layout. In the old townhouse, the kitchen was open on the dining room and the yard and provided sightlines to the living room and the entrance hall. Due to this central and open location, you could catch glimpses of the cook at work but also hear noise from the pans and smell the aroma of dishes being prepared. The kitchen held profes-sional equipment and appliances made of stainless steel, which gave it a professional character. However, the domestic spatial layout invited the teenagers and caregivers to stop by countless times each day, to take leftover food from the fridge or put a coffee mug in the sink. In this way, the kitchen held an institutional ambiguity between professional and domestic site.

For the new building, the architects and caregivers insisted that the kitchen remain part of the group's circulation. However, the consensus was not so smooth. Josie, the cook, had precise requirements for practical details so the kitchen could meet her need for storage, cleaning, cutting, baking, as well as socializing, all in the same spot. As perhaps goes without saying, this was far from easy. Even if the kitchen was first and foremost Josie's workspace, it had become too crowded in the townhouse for her to prepare meals with the intense traffic that disturbed her workflow (figure 10). In other words, hanging out in the kitchen worked too well for her to cook without too much disturbance. She asked to close off the kitchen, but this was not an option to the team nor the architects, who wanted to maintain conditions of togetherness. The new kitchen arrangements ended in a compromise: the baking part was left open, but walking through it was not possible anymore. In this way, the kitchen became semi-open. The low wall delimiting the kitchen in the townhouse was rebuilt as a larger bar in the new building, inviting its occupants to sit down or to hang out in that area, away from the food preparation area (figure 9). In the new building, the kitchen's appeal was balanced with the help of the bar's material layout.

Figure 9: Birds-eye view of the living spaces in the new building, with a sofa in the corner and people hanging around the bar.

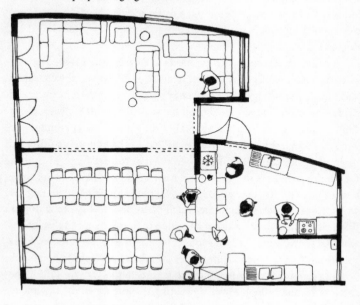

Figure 10: Birds-eye view of the kitchen in the house, with people hanging around the cook.

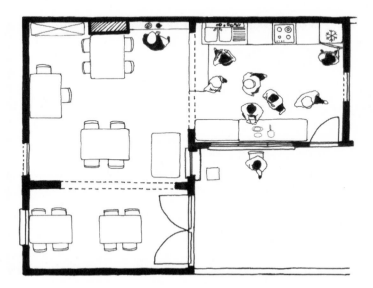

Now, I puzzled over these spatial details, but I never saw the kitchen work quite as well when Josie was absent. The kitchen's spatial organization gave her a central position, which helped make it a central spot. A round lady with mellow movements, exact gestures, and a deep quiet voice, Josie's presence mediated our informal encounters with the kitchen.[10] In interviews, the teens told me how often they went to see her, as did the caregivers. One of them shared that, "by speaking

---

10   In the field of medical sociology, Martin (2016) draws analogies between an open kitchen in a support center for cancer and the spaces of cafés: both working sites provide affordances for informal encounters, for sharing a place with strangers as much as more familiar others. Here, the open kitchen was so tightly connected with the person of the cook that strangeness had very few chances to survive among attendants.

with her, we are in the group, with the teens who are often around the kitchen." Sometimes I also glimpsed more intimate interactions with Josie, like when one came whispering to her, or helped her refasten an earring as it loosened while she cooked. She was a caregiver, too, but of a different kind. She gave care without it being officially recognized as such. She never left 'her' kitchen, but she noticed who had eaten or not, or who had not had enough, and who had helped with the dishes. She whispered her observations to the caregivers but never addressed the teens concerned directly. Josie embraced the ambiguity of her position as a caregiver. The team invited her to attend their weekly meeting to share her views with them, but she refused. Only once, after settling in the new building, did she attend a more important meeting for aligning with the new organization. I heard her snoring after half an hour. She did not seem interested in more formal discussions about the teens, institutional matters, the care or therapy. Just as her semi-open kitchen, she remained an institutional ambiguity, a mediator of informal encounters. Without their ambiguous position in relation to their institutional purpose, the 'hanging out' social dynamic would most probably not have occurred as such. The open kitchen, the cook, and the movement around them formed a suggestion that stirred things up, scrambling daily routines. Together with spatial elements that permitted more relaxed bodily positions, the kitchen and the cook helped our familiar webs to unfold by hanging out without much overt involvement in activity.

Material suggestions

During the first few weeks of my fieldwork and when moving to the new building, clustering hotspots, contact adjustments and hanging out manifested as some of the ways in which familiarity was enacted in everyday care. In particular, those stories helped me better understand how the living spaces contributed to the forming of attachments. They demonstrated the suggestive importance of the material affordances of such spaces. By no means would their spatial arrangements invite clear and straightforward (inter)personal accommodations. Of course, the living spaces proposed apparent functional uses, like sitting at a table to eat. But they also left room to maneuver as they suggested informal and (inter)personal accommodations, like hanging out in the kitchen. Instead of a strictly functional place that explicitly stated who did what and where, these living spaces afforded the teens and caregivers to familiarize thanks to material suggestions that were open-ended and ambiguous. Hotspots and their objects, such as games, benches, or the semi-open kitchen, attracted others to join without overt invitation, prompting participants to cluster or hang out. Hotspots incited them to engage in ambiguous play and to space their bodies to better deal with simmering tensions. The presence of many available objects supported the adjustment of contact when addressing another indirectly. The articulation of rooms did so too, whether by exchanging discreet glances through sharp sight lines, or by negotiating one's presence through distance adjustments. In these ways, the living spaces were suggestive since their invitations were open-ended with different possibilities. They left room for ambiguities insofar as everyone's engagement could be tailored to a way that better suited them in a present situation, when doing something, addressing someone, adopting a casual attitude, going somewhere, or being near someone else. This was how the living spaces fostered familiar bonds. Perhaps their 'institutional ambiguity', being both a domestic setting and a workplace, was best palpable in the case of the kitchen, its layout and its cook. They stirred up informal encounters while enticing us to hang out together. In sum, the living spaces, with their hotspots and available things, rooms articulations and corners for withdrawing, resting elements and central kitchen, provided affordances that worked as 'material suggestions'.

What I call material suggestions underlined a mode of moderate, soft attraction that characterized the affordances of those spatial arrangements. These affordances worked in a specific manner: they did not furnish straightforward propositions, but what could be done with them was quite open-ended. In other words, for the living spaces or its objects to invite users to experience informal contacts and attitudes, and to develop personal acquaintances, their affordances had to remain suggestive. A crucial dimension of the notion of affordance is that of perception: an environment affords someone's action when that person perceives some of its specific features. Thus, an affordance is ecological: neither a property of a physical surrounding, nor a subjective property, it points both ways, to the reciprocity at stake in the interaction between an organism and an environment (Gibson 1986: 129). In the context of the day center, this reciprocity worked through suggestions and possible responses to them. For instance, narrow sightlines incited discreet glances without imposing a gaze on the viewer, nor on the object of their attention. Such affordances of space remained unclear and suggestive because they induced actions – a cluster, a glimpse, a bodily positioning, a move to another spot, or a move towards a smell, etc. – without forcing those outcomes. I'm not saying that the living space's affordances were not or hardly perceptible. Their opacity was of a different kind from that of incomprehensible objects whose design gives no clues – or sometimes false clues – on how to use them, causing everyday frustrations (Norman 1998). Here, unclear affordances did not entail misunderstanding, but contingency: their open-ended and ambiguous character presented occasions for personal convenience, offering the possibility to attune to what happened in the moment. This way, the living spaces' suggestions allowed a youth's personality to form by diffusing itself in the surrounding, recalling Thévenot's words (2001: 77) about the 'attached personality' that takes shape with familiar usages.

In the context of a psychotherapeutic practice, the notion of material suggestions raises the problem of influence on the people one seeks to care for. Since material spaces suggest certain ways of doing, they influence mundane interactions with them and between teens and caregivers. The common understanding of 'suggestion' assumes a psychological process that brings an idea to the mind when someone or something gives hints or inklings, without plain or direct explanation. Suggestions in the waking state, psychology scientists acknowledge, are not especially verbal. An environment, an object, a gesture or a wink can be suggestive as well, in a deliberate manner or not.[11] Due to its insinuative, tempting, seductive or prompting character, the practice of suggestion has acquired a bad reputation. It underwent a controversial history because it contradicts the ideal of freedom of the human subject, who is supposed to be autonomous and rational and equipped with free will.[12]

The material suggestions I identified with the living spaces did not presume that freedom meant autonomy without constraint. Rather, they brought attention to the contingency of their influence, and how it created different possibilities to act. Not only were these suggestions contingent upon their open-ended character, leaving ambiguity as to a teen's inclination to the possible uses of an arrangement, but such responses

---

11   Studies on the effects of suggestion have spanned many fields, among others, placebo experiments, school learning and, more disconcerting, the justice system. See Michael, Garry & Kirsch (2012).

12   Suggestion sparked fierce debate during the time of Freud. He rejected hypnosis techniques and transformed their recourse to suggestion into 'transference'. This concept purified the patients' life experiences from its randomness, and brought it back into an inner symptom with which the analyst could work in ways Freud saw as controllable. According to him, assuming that suggestions have potency in the therapeutic relationship would have dismissed the idea that symptoms come from inside the patient and, in the same move, it would have failed to align with scientific legitimacy (Stengers 1992).

Furthermore, the material suggestions that I observed in the day center are reminiscent of 'nudging' practices. By making small changes in an existing environment, a nudge gently pushes someone's decision-making. Nudging has raised a lot of ethical debates, specifically as whether it undermines or strengthens people's autonomy (Vugts et al. 2020). However, although here suggestions invite certain doings while remaining open to an array of possibilities, analysis through the lens of 'attachment' poses the problem differently. The concept presumes that individuals are not either free or alienated, but that they're caught in various reciprocal driving forces when entering in relation with other beings (human or not). These forces occur on the middle path of the 'faire-faire', that is, as much 'to make one do' as 'causing to be done'. Consequently, the moral and political problem is not to gauge whether an individual's autonomy is infringed or not, but rather to better distinguish good or bad attachments in the details of someone's relations. For this argument about the concept of attachment, see Latour (1999).

also impacted how caregivers would attune to them. When Rachid nego-
tiated his degree of distance to the adolescents at a particular spot, in a
particular moment, the influence was exerted through spatial mediation
from patient to therapist, not only the other way around. When material
suggestions work in such a contingent manner, they diffuse influence on
others in countless ways, shattering the premise of a one-way vector tar-
geted at someone. These discreet, ordinary and unruly forces allow one
to disrupt the asymmetrical relationships inherent to care work. While
teens were often tempted or drawn into a meandering flow of ambiguous
suggestions, they could easily dodge them as well. They also influenced
the team in how they responded, either with personal accommodation,
or with resistance to it.

In my view, it was because material suggestions enabled such contingent influences that they were constitutive of the care work. Far
from entailing a mere permissiveness or freedom, these suggestions
enabled teens and caregivers to familiarize while better dealing with the
discomfort of institutional pressure. Indeed, the close relationships that
caregivers sought to incite were often not easy for the teens to engage
with. Simply being in the day center already constituted an institutional
pressure to participate in community life, activities, and more formal
therapy (interviews, medication). The teens I met were highly sensitive
to the ambiguity between being with others and being burdened by their
expectations. They retreated when they felt one had tried to impose a
certain behavior upon them, particularly teenagers who had already
frequented many institutions. The atmosphere in the living space was
highly volatile. It could pass from electric agitation to dead calm, and
hence asked adjustment of teens who needed company or tranquility.
In interviews, most of the teens evoked how much they did not feel the
duties of "staying here" or "going there". While describing their typical
day, the teens' words, at first unsettling, insisted on these contingencies:
"I happen to […]", "it depends on […]", "either [I go here], or [there]", "if
[someone is there/doing something], then I go towards [them]", etc.

This dependency on circumstance frames familiarity as a form of attachment that sprouts when someone tests what might please them in
a given situation, in the moment. The person focuses less on themself,

on an object, or on a genre, but with this form of attachment it is the appropriate moment or situation that is pertinent (Hennion 2007: 110–111). In this sense, the material suggestions foster familiarity as a highly opportunistic attachment. I do not say that they remove the discomfort of institutional pressure, persistently at stake in the diffuse influences when caregivers and adolescents adjusted their attitudes. But had the spatial arrangements or the team imposed more formal interactions or assumed intentions, making teenagers feel a duty to socialize, the latter would hardly familiarize in such informal and contingent ways. They would hardly create these early personal attachments in the middle of everyday objects and casual attitudes. Consequently, caregivers' informal knowledge would also dissolve, since they would lose the possibility of progressively perceiving how each teenager responded to the suggestions of the living spaces, and to their contingent influence.

Chapter 3
Involvement in workshops

"There, we had a spatial problem." Marion, a caregiver, signaled to me at the end of the first month of fieldwork, calling my attention to workshop spaces in the old house. She went on:

> One Wednesday a month, we have two workshops that should be done in L'Annexe [a room for creative activities] at the same time. Thus last time, we found ourselves doing a Creation workshop in the dining room. It was horrible! It was not good at all: the frame... the place's resonance... well, it was not framing.
> I seized it: When you say, 'not framing', what is it exactly?
> Marion: We didn't have the material we needed. So we brought some [from L'Annexe], but this limits the expression work we asked them [teens] to do. And for them it was not a place where we usually put ourselves in our bubble and work. This is a community place [le communautaire], where we usually eat our meals. We have access to glasses, to coffee, and so on, and not to the material we need to be at hand. And the resonance, and the light are not the same. There is something less calm, less cocooned, that helps less to put themselves in their bubble.

The living spaces were quite good at suggesting familiar bonds, but when it came to involving teens in focused activities, except maybe for a cooking workshop, these material spaces were certainly not models of an ideal configuration. On the contrary, here a Creation workshop was made hardly possible since the spaces did not provide the right materials available at hand. And their light and resonance prevented participants from applying themselves to what they were supposed to do. So certain conditions were needed to frame the activity in ways that enabled teenagers to 'put themselves in their bubble', to get involved in doing it. Marion's words hint at a form of attachment occurring in everyday activities, when the adolescents were caught up in a sort of connection to what they did. Her words also indicate that the possibility to create such a bubble was linked to certain conditions, among which the space played a key role in switching participants to another state. The spatial problem that Marion raised opens a path for turning to the material spaces for activities, and for tackling these questions: How does teenagers' involvement take shape, with its successes and failures, during the care work? And how do the material spaces of activities provide conditions for these involvements?

In this chapter I probe how teens' affinities took shape in workshops in relation to their spatial settings. I first portray what an 'involvement' in practice is and the role it plays for the care work. I then turn to several issues that add more layers to the picture: the 'framing' of activities, the uncertain character of such attachments, the adjustments they require when facing school tasks, their call to bodily senses, and teens' disinvolvement from a planned activity. This ensemble of stories led me to see that workshop spaces together with caregivers' techniques facilitated teenagers' passage from indifference to greater involvement into what they were proposed to do. These transitions could succeed or fail, especially since teens involvement was uncertain and unstable. However faint and ephemeral, teens' passage to and from their involvement in workshops were key daily events to the team, who could then work with each teen's personal traits, difficulties and possibilities.

Relating 'involvement'

To begin with, where, when, and how did I discern the 'involvement' of teens in activities in the care work? The team proposed a repertoire of activities that might be of interest to the teens. When newcomers arrived in the center, they were offered to choose what activity they wanted to do on a weekly timetable (table 1). They then scheduled their choice for a two-week trial period. Presenting the timetable to them was a way to ask: what do you like? Its repertoire was designed to appeal to tastes adolescents would most likely have already developed. Not surprisingly, sports or video games were largely triumphant over knitting. The teens went to their activities each morning and afternoon. In every morning meeting, the team reported on the happenings in the previous day's workshops. Often these observations had already been partially shared at informal moments, as caregivers interacted in their shared office space.

Table 1: Timetable of a weekly program.

	Monday	**Tuesday**	**Wednesday**	**Thursday**	**Friday**
8.30-9h	Arrival & breakfast				
9.30	Welcome meeting				
10h	Speaking group 'Stylistique'/ Board games/ Role-play therapy	Pedagogical workshop/ Sport / Video games	Cooking atelier/ Horse riding/ Sport	Pedagogical workshop/ Radio workshop	Clay atelier/ Hip-hop dance/ Climbing
12.30	Lunch / informal time / appointments				
14.15	Pedagogical workshop/ Mosaic/ 'Introduce me your city'	Creative workshop/ Music/ Writing atelier	Pedagogical workshop/ Cultural discoveries/ Photography	Community meeting	Body workshop (single gender)
16.30	Snack & closing				

But I soon realized, caregivers used a plethora of verbs to tell of the teens' responses when they reported stories about recent workshop sessions. The teens "got/were involved", "engaged themselves", "participated", "invested themselves", etc. It was a bit perplexing for me to figure out, after hearing all these terms, how I would follow a single conceptual line. This became even more disquieting when I discussed the matter with Ingrid, a caregiver who wondered how each of these terms, once translated from their common use into an ethnographic text, would be burdened with connotations. An 'engagement' would point to a long-term commitment, with the requirement of making a pledge, and less to being caught up in an ongoing situation. Although teens who attended a session were called 'participants', the word 'participation' puts too strong an emphasis on their input when taking an active part. And 'to invest oneself' conjures the psychoanalytic tradition. There, it supposes an analogy between psychic operations and nervous functioning, to detect how patients invest their energetic discharges towards an object or a representation. The term 'investment' assumes that forces only come from people, whereas I'm interested in the conditions distributed within material and social environments. They, too, exert forces and reveal weaknesses. So Ingrid and I came to agree that the term 'involvement' was the best candidate for reporting the states that caregivers sought to induce in practice, and that I could describe as an ethnographer.

Indeed, such involvement was less a normative prerequisite to which teens should be able to answer, as if it relied solely on them, or as if their lack of involvement would incur the team's disapproval of their reason for being in the center.[1] The teens' involvement was everything but an individual duty. Instead it required attempts from the team to enfold them in an ongoing activity, with a diffuse power at stake when trying to lure them. In practice, the caregivers noticed how the adolescents paid attention during an activity, the things they came to use,

---

1   This tension is crucial among therapeutic and social workers who resist the (implicit or explicit) injunction that care receivers must involve themselves personally in order to receive support (Rafanell i Orra 2011: 159).

the gestures they made, when they expressed pleasure, emerging ideas, hesitations, or aversions, or had exchanges with other participants. The term 'involvement' (in French, *'implication'*) depicts these various ways of engaging oneself in interactions with things and others. To me, it resonates with Goffman's work. His examination of 'involvement' targets the perceivable, verbal or non-verbal responses of a participant who, in practice, "gives, or withdraws from giving, his concerted attention to some activity at hand [...]", implying "a certain closeness between the individual and the object of involvement, a certain overt engrossment on the part of the one who is involved" (Goffman 1963: 43).[2] This notion, then, helps to convey those back and forth movements in interaction and attitude that showed how participants became more or less captivated by an activity, swept away indifference or returned to it, came to dedicate themselves within workshops, retreated to the margins of disinvolvement, or turned towards other involvements outside of the main activity – but without assuming that these responses came from individual teenagers. In the day center, to induce and enhance these movements, gestures, attention, concentration, or concerns of the adolescents was a daily challenge for the team.

But how exactly did teens' involvements play a role in their care work? I kept being struck by the manner in which the caregivers reported every-

---

2   The notion of 'involvement' reaches much further throughout Goffman's work. The sociologist first draws the contours of the concept in his doctoral thesis in 1955. He casts it as a "subtle mixture of spontaneity and calculation" needed to make an interaction succeed (Winkin (2016 [1988]): 93, my translation). In *Behavior in Public Places* (1963), Goffman underlines the normative character of the non-verbal communication and gestures used in reacting to an encounter (35). After discussing the bodily aspect of involvement, the author adds more layers to the concept: "To be engaged in an occasioned activity means to sustain some kind of cognitive and affective engrossment in it, some mobilization of one's psychobiological resources: in short, it means to be *involved* in it." (Ibid: 36, original emphasis). Goffman insists that involvement always occurs within a situation, where normativity is at stake in a group that use its own idioms of involvement. In this way, he conceptualizes a 'self' that is situational, crafted through involvements in interactions.

day stories about workshops. Their tones and gestures evoked the moments they had experienced, making the rest of the team feel as though it was happening on the spot. As with familiar bonds, the teens' involvement in activities was noticeable in very small responses and discreet interactions. Let's listen to Etienne who, during a morning team meeting, talked about a workshop he had led in the studio of a small radio station:

> There, the space is divided in two rooms: the technical room and the one with the microphones. [...] One room is where we play the recordings and the other one for the live broadcast, where we [caregivers and teenagers] sometimes improvise. A small red light switches on and – Hop! It's our turn to speak! We go on air! So obviously, it is not always easy. ... Karl and Dorian were in the technical room, so they played things with a big console. ... Well, they were well caught up in that play, with the technical and computing things. Karl did it with this very serious position, about the technical features, a bit like in the cooking workshop, when he takes very seriously his responsibility, very assertive. He is good in that role. On the contrary, he will never come to speak into the microphones. There is no way for him. It is like in the cooking workshop, he won't go to speak to the cashier at the grocery.

Not only did caregivers report on a teen's involvement, but they also compared it between different activities, or between different parts of an activity with its respective material and technical settings. Etienne was struck by Karl's assertive involvement in technical tasks when he captained the radio console, and by his avoidance of spontaneous ones when he wouldn't dare speak in a live broadcast. Noticing this was supported by previous observations in the cooking workshop, where part of the setting, dedicated to the preparation of dinner, entailed technical tasks in the kitchen and another, like speaking to the cashier, required spontaneity in front of others. Workshops were diverse and each happened in specific settings, inside and outside the center. Teenagers responded to distinct settings in their own way. According to what they were more inclined to do, they would easily enter one state while dodging others. Caregivers noticed how it went and learned to know each youth when recognizing similar involvements and aversions, and they shared these clues with the team.

Thus, caregivers related teens' involvement in the double senses of 'relating': while giving an account of what they had noticed, they also connected it to other observations or information that was within their reach. In doing so, caregivers tried to better see what the youth's logic and sensibilities were, and the accompanying forces and difficulties. The team did not seek the strong commitment of an adolescent in a particular workshop. Instead they compared the various ways that teens got involved with and disengaged from different situations at hand. Other caregivers also related stories, as they recognized these same clues or contested them – sometimes relating as well to occurrences that happened during informal time in the living spaces. In this manner, they built, expanded, and reinforced their informal knowledge of each teenager. Whoever attended team meetings or hung around in their office was quickly aware of that informal knowledge, and was often drawn to help build it.

It was slowly becoming clear to me that caregivers' acquaintance with each youth enabled them to notice unpredictable changes among them. Workshops were diverse and put to the test the particular inclinations and aversions of each adolescent. On an everyday basis, caregivers narrated how workshops ran into snags due to personal, often emotional and relational difficulties, such as conflicts, distresses, fatigue, refusals, and so on. But they could also be pleasantly surprised by incremental changes in youth involvement. I heard in a team meeting how Karina, who always showed a will to perform tasks perfectly, started to relax, let go, ask more questions, say things more fluidly. "It starts", a caregiver recounted: "We feel something is becoming different in workshops." Her colleagues recognized that Karina had changed in the manner she got involved. This change became a common concern that spread across the staff, all agreeing that they were better off supporting her in furthering a more relaxed involvement. I also heard about teens usually boiling over when in a group, who became more able to hold themselves back from messing things up. Caregivers commonly mentioned bodily movements or contacts in those changes. They mentioned how Nadia, a rather stiff, inhibited youth, came to respond with laugh and smile in dance or massage workshops, or how one day girls "completely unleashed themselves" in games that demanded moving around and jumping. Caregivers also noted changes in verbal involvement, as when participants "take their places" in bringing their knowledge of a topic to the rest of the group. It seems from all this that, day after day, meeting after meeting, alongside the familiarity each adolescent wove in the center, their involvement in workshops was a vital constituent of the sociotherapeutic work. In the ongoing practice, teens' responses in activities did not merely provide the team with informal knowledge, but also reshaped it, with surprising changes that called for adjusting the care work with them.

Framing uncertain attachments

Now, when caregivers spoke about teens' involvement, their focus went beyond the persons. Their discussion touched, too, to the "frame" that Marion evoked about the Creation Workshop: the material setting that could encourage or hinder it. What does it mean, in practice, to frame participants' involvement in an activity? This question brings our attention back to the spatial conditions of workshops and leads us to discern more nuances about that form of attachment.

Workshops, as diverse as they were, worked much better – and sometimes could only work – with precise arrangements that fitted the type of activity. The move to the new building brought these requirements into sharper relief. It offered caregivers the occasion to arrange certain rooms with greater specificity. One such rearrangement occurred with a room on the first floor in the old townhouse. Due to lack of space, it served as a multipurpose room and was arranged with minimal and flexible objects, like foldable chairs, tables with wheels, a closed storage unit, a movable TV screen, and computers at the back of the room. Two of the activities that happened in this room were named *Cidébat* (in French, a mix of '*cinéma*' and '*débat*') and Writing Play. Both required caregivers to quickly arrange the room to create different settings: chairs randomly facing the screen for the first, and a big central table where everybody could sit without being too close for the second. After having moved to the big new building, however, keeping both workshops in a single multipurpose room proved absurd after just a few sessions. Ingrid, the caregiver in charge of both activities, recounted to me how they tried to move the writing workshop from a small room in the middle of the ground floor corridor to another one, located upstairs, whose "atmosphere was more suitable .... brighter... [with] views on the garden and on tree [... and for] a youth who sometimes wants to sit alone for writing, a table at the back." This room, with its light, views, and possibilities for distance adjustments, better matched ideal conditions for writing. The activity's displacement from one room to another allowed the downstairs room to be dedicated to workshops meant to direct the teens' collective attention towards a screen, like Cidébat or video games. There, Ingrid explained, the teens' involvement was greatly improved after adding some lounge chairs, a blind for the light, a few movie and game posters, and DVDs on the shelves.

When I asked her how precisely those changes of material setting affected the running of workshops, Ingrid was quick to answer, "Then we really could 'make a group' with teens!" She underlined how these conditions for the group were inescapably entwined with specific forms of concentration. I had to attend the activities to understand what this was all about. Next Tuesday, we started the Writing Play session by sitting around the central table with Sabine, an external artist, who gave us some constraints for playing with our writing. We spread to different tables, some participants withdrawing further in corners. We spent around half an hour focusing on our own pages, every now and then letting our attention drift to the sky and the foliage beyond the windowpanes. You could have heard a fly buzz while we were concentrating on our words. We then gathered back at the main table, read our pieces aloud, and shared comments on the choices of words, rhythm, metaphors, or about a wider scope of unexpected issues raised by the texts' content. Passing through to this second moment implied a switch, as each of us departed from our paper and went back to the group.

Doing the Cidébat also implied a switch in attention, but it did so quite otherwise. The small room downstairs was far less open to a range of suggestions. Here, walls surrounded us as we randomly placed our chairs in front of the screen. Bodies were much closer. The twilight enhanced this closeness, as well as our attention towards the movie. During the screening, Ingrid sometimes paused it and turned the light on, in the aim of launching short debates on what was going on in certain scenes. The switch between focus on the film and exchanges within the group provided occasions to encourage teenagers' reflexivity, not only about the object of appreciation but about broader issues as well.

The two rooms, each in their specific manner, framed distinctive forms of participant concentration. These differences brought into relief, too, two different ways to switch their attention from a greater absorption in the movie, towards group exchanges and relations with the other participants. The passage between these different states was at the core of teenagers' involvement.

But it must be said that framing the right conditions for participants' involvement in an activity did not always rely so heavily on the specific features of a material setting. Gaël, a caregiver, specified to me that going outside remained crucial to the care practice, for it relied on "the infrastructures available in everyday life", such as public transport, places or facilities that everyone used. Often, though, going outside led to more messiness. One of the most open-ended activities in terms of spatial organization was called "Introduce me to your city". It could happen anywhere in Brussels, but not in just any way. It relied on a basic framework: for each session, a youth chose a place in Brussels that mattered to him or her, and guided the others there. The teen received a camera to use during the outing, and some of the pictures would later be displayed in the center. So the setting encompassed no less than Brussels, its public transport, its meeting spots, public infrastructure for walking or resting, a camera, and occasionally a map. And its framework relied on the teenagers' previous attachments to a place, the group's preparation for the outing, and the guiding youth. I joined some of these trips, and heard plenty of accounts upon the return of others. These made clear that, even though the framework sounded easy, often its actual happening was not. It sometimes became embroiled, for instance, when a young guide was confused about which way to go, or when other participants resisted or even utterly refused to visit certain areas. Despite these disruptions, caregivers related many fruitful sessions of that workshop since it often produced moments where meeting one another was possible in ways that were not with ateliers constricted to a place. Since traveling and walk was the main activity, other contacts could be established and things said that were possible only thanks to this situation of being in motion in changing surroundings.[3] In this workshop participants weren't captivated by an object, but rather drawn into place exploration, and this sowed easier chats along the way. This experience relied far less on accurate spatial conditions, and more on a thin practical framework that left a margin for unexpected events.

What becomes confusing, here, is that the porous aspect of these conditions in outside places makes you wonder whether teens' involvement, after all, could happen anywhere, whatever the material environment providing a frame for it. As the stories above witness, the importance of spatial organization depends of course on the specific kind of involvement caregivers seek to create. But the question of the 'anywhere' of activities limited caregivers' framing work. The threshold of minimal conditions for an activity to be considered therapeutic work remained under debate among them. Going to the cinema was one of the outside activities that heated that debate because, some caregivers argued, it could be merely 'occupational'. This meant that such a minimal frame would lead to simply pass time with teens, probably giving some rest to the activity leaders. But going to the cinema, other caregivers asserted, substantially contributed to the sociotherapeutic work insofar as they chose movies with teens about topics of their concern, organized the outing with them, and opened discussions about them. In short, they

---

3   The meditative experience of walking has spilled the ink of a fair number of writers and philosophers, although most often when practiced in solitude. Ingold and Vergunst's (2008) collection of ethnographies explores walking as a social activity, but I haven't found in it an account that addresses how walking with others would ease a chat, compared to more formal face-to-face interactions.

went to the cinema in a way that further solicited the teenagers' personal involvement and reflexivity. Caregivers' framing then built upon existing activities with material settings, such as a trailer, walking trajectory, ticket desk, screening room with its bleachers, or a nearby café. Framing the activity with this setting intensified a little bit what most of us do when going to see a movie. Their minimal framing took advantage of a mundane activity and amplified these activities to foster reflexive mindsets. By doing so, they turned that activity into therapeutic work.[4]

You won't be surprised, will you, to learn that the adolescents could resist and renegotiate a frame well. A noteworthy incident of this kind occurred during the Cidébat workshop. In the small dark room, remember, Ingrid interrupted the screening and turned the light on to switch the attention from the film to group exchange. But at some point of the session, Jimmy started to complain about these switches. He wanted to "be in the movie like as usual", he pleaded, meaning without being interrupted by pauses. Although in this workshop the movie served as an occasion for debate, to be engrossed by the plot was also necessary for his involvement, to enjoy the screening and simultaneously to make up his mind about it. Jimmy's complaint prompted all participants to revise the frame. After discussion, they decided to keep the pauses for debate after longer screening moments, long enough to be able to 'enter' into the movie again. So the framing of activity did not only help one put oneself in a bubble, as Marion pointed out. It was also about setting up the conditions to amplify any activity most of us do from time to time, like going to the movies or watching a film at home, in ways that better triggered participants' reflexivity. This reflexivity, as Jimmy reminded us, could also pertain to the frame of the activity itself.

---

4   To some caregivers, a minimal frame turns the activities and their objects into 'therapeutic mediations'. This means they foster a subjective appropriation of the medium by the patient. I don't share this understanding, first because such mediations through objects seem to target patients' symbolic speech, and I observed plenty of practical interactions that came to be relevant for care as well. Second, I base my analysis on the notion of attachment that carries a different, more social and material idea of 'mediation' (Hennion 2015 [1993]); but see the note about it in the introduction).

Looking back at these articulations about the 'framing' of activities
– from the switches in participants' attention with the specific arrangements of Writing Play and Cidébat, to the minimal conditions of outings,
and the reflexivity all these framings were designed to trigger – teens'
involvement now appears as a highly uncertain form of attachment. Indeed, I recognize in these framings the words of Hennion, Gomart and
Maisonneuve (2000: 181). While regarding taste as an accomplishment
in a practice in which attachments develop, they emphasize how amateurs create the right conditions to warm up a situation, and better feel
if they like an object or not. Such a creation of conditions could involve
the setting of a concert hall, but so would the gestures of a wine connois-
seur handling their glass and smelling it before drinking. In any case, it
is important to note that these meticulous assessments occur on a middle path: it is about actively making an affinity emerge, and being passively caught in it. In other words, when an attachment takes shape, it
is an event that occurs *between* the taster and the thing, without locating
the action in either one of them. Tasters may notice more refined differences, which intensify their feelings and perceptions, while the object
deploys its qualities to them. Hennion says that these events happen in
a reflexive mode (in French, *'cela se passe'*) that concerns the taster ("well,
this music/wine is not so bad...") as much as the object that is able to respond, interrupt, or surprise them (Hennion 2009: 63). And it is because
amateurs' appreciation occurs on such a middle path that they remain
uncertain during reflexive moments.

Similarly, in the day center, the framing of activities offered conditions for participants' involvement in ways that their appreciations could
be tested, especially since it encouraged reflexivity. Although material
spaces provide conditions for possible involvement, it happens without
guarantee, because the action doesn't come from a person or a thing, instead tracing a middle path between them. Of course, beyond the material and practical frame with which participants engage in the moment,
many other mediators cultivate one's appreciation before and during an
activity. In Hennion's theory of attachment, too, the creation of conditions does not only belong to the isolated moment of tasting, to the interactions between tasters and things, but it also relies on an extended flow

of attachments (to previous experiences; to a body having been trained over time; to collectives, their judgments, and controversies; to other objects and places, etc.). This was clear as well in the case of the workshop "Introduce me to your city". Its framework was largely dependent on the teenagers' previous attachments to a place. So the team also considered the appreciations, and sometimes the passions, that teenagers had already developed before arriving. Nevertheless, what caregivers mostly did was to frame teens' possible involvement in the moment, on the uncertain pathways towards accomplishing an activity. They experienced it together with them on the spot and related it to their colleagues thereafter.

This is not a classroom

Knowing these uncertain paths, it turned out that workshops in the care practice did not aim at achieving impressive performances. The day center was a transitional place where the caregivers aimed at helping the teenagers regain stability in their lives. For most of them, this meant going back to school or engaging in professional projects. This was not a ready-made path. On the contrary, most of the teens had gone to many different schools and repeated years several times. All of them had dropped out of school for a while. A small group of caregivers, along with some teachers and artists, set up *La Porte Bleue*, a pedagogical workshop that attempted to reinitiate the learning of skills. Most of these were academic skills, which the adolescents anticipated negatively. For that specific workshop, the team mingled psychotherapeutic and pedagogic practices in order to try to reinvigorate teens' interest and rebuild their self-confidence, before tackling cognitive skills. Retrieving pleasure in learning was central for enabling the teens to dare to try it. Next to schoolwork, the team offered projects based on the production of artifacts of all kinds. This way, they hoped to pique the adolescents' interest and to drive their willingness to acquire new knowledge.

Teens' involvement in sessions at La Porte Bleue were thus granted a special status, for they might extend great promise but also deep disappointments. Kevin's story remains a striking one. He was only twelve, but had already spent years living in residential institutions for teens, or on the streets – where he happened to return some nights. Most of the time, he was unable to sit still. Yet for several months, his involvement in certain workshops suggested that he could find a sustainable project. As his interest in these activities solidified, he nearly did. One of the things he liked to do was to make models. So the team of La Porte Bleue started with that. Then model making became a vehicle for learning school subjects such as mathematics and history. During a staff meeting, Maud, the caregiver in charge of this workshop, related that it had worked quite well, but that it was not sufficient:

> When he works on the model, I just give him a bit admiring attention, but without intervention. Then he's in his bubble and he can slow down. Because, he always wants to hurry. ... But then we should not only offer him these bubbles. Which work to do with him now, for a long-term perspective?

The team reviewed several possible institutions and schools and concluded that an internship would be a better track for him. Maud found a place that would have been great: a center for rehabilitating birds located two houses from the day center. Kevin was delighted by this idea. He loved having contact with animals. Other caregivers had noticed him becoming quieter, watchful, and responsive when caring for horses. And the director of the bird rehabilitation center had agreed on the internship. And then, quite suddenly, Kevin disappeared. He somehow returned to street life for longer. For more than a month he didn't come back to the center, nor did he return to his residential institution. Caregivers were worried about the risks he ran in his homeless lifestyle. They sometimes met him in the neighborhood, where he came to give some news. But after having been reported to the police as a runaway for more than three weeks, Kevin wasn't legally allowed to continue his stay in the center or to start the internship. The term 'disenchanted' does not begin to describe how caregivers felt about this acute disappointment. They were daunted. Even though Kevin's involvement with models and animals opened a track for him, other forces made him drop out of it.

His story leaves little doubt about the vulnerable aspect of teens' involvement in the pedagogical workshop, which creates possible life projects for them. The care work was to keep trying to create a path without any guarantee of success. This was also the case for most of the other teenagers I eventually saw going back to school or to an internship. Those paths never appeared without pitfalls.

The space of La Porte Bleue thus was to enable teaching, training and raising interest among participants while dealing with the fragile aspects of resuming schoolwork and setting up a long-term project. In doing so, it could not in any way be designed as a standard classroom. Rather, it was a protected space, set a bit apart from the group's daily movements. No one could come there when sessions were occurring. No trainee, no ethnographer. It was only after having heard about that mysterious place for months that I went there with Maud, who gave me a guided tour. We walked to another large townhouse, two streets from the old building. She took me up to two rooms on the first floor, whose windows gave a view on gardens, yet without exposing the viewer to gazes from outside. While Maud told me how sessions happened there, I identified different ways in which the spaces provided conditions for trying to involve teens in learning, while tending to their apprehensions.

A first way related to the awakening of curiosity. Lots of objects were displayed all over both rooms. Collages, brushes, maps, files, a guitar, pictures, little notes, sculptures, a sewing machine, drawings, pinned sketches and framed paintings, and so forth, filled the spaces. All these things witnessed what had been made, or what was in the middle of being achieved. They were disposed with that sort of inevitable slight messiness that belongs to artworks in process. Though one room was devoted to schoolwork and the other to artistic activities, both looked more like art studios. They gave few clues about learning spaces, such as a blackboard painted on a wall, or a world map. The displayed objects were not left there because of a lack of storage space elsewhere. They played a role in practice, as Maud told me, especially when a youth discovered them:

I always do a first interview with a new youth in these rooms, because I want them to see it, to feel it. Even if it's messy, at least something would speak to them. It is a good indication when one says: 'hey,
what's that?' And when nothing special catches their attention, you
think: 'ouch, it is still complicated'. But where I'm sure to draw attention, it's when we pass to the artistic activities room. I show them the
three paintings placed under glass [figure 11]. These surely interest
them, without doubt, because they are beautiful, they're well done.
And because it's something within their reach: a drawing, it is easier
to do than study electricity, algebra or French. ... There, you can feel
how you will start to work with a youth, by being attentive to the way
they take up the space: what do they look at, what are they are going
to touch.

Maud described a technique that I understood as a 'curiosity trial'. The
exhibition of these objects was not explicit. They were subtly left here
and there within the mess. Their valorization was moderated, without
great means, without glorification. These objects didn't seem to be meant
for display. They were however beautiful and well done, or at least they
could 'speak to' teenagers. To an anthropologist's ears, Maud's description of what these artworks did recalls Gell's theory about the agency of
art (1998). To him, it is the technical virtuosity of the object that trig-
gers a personal relationship with its observer, who in turn may be fascinated by it and in this way enter into relation with the artist. The beautiful and well-done objects displayed in the workshop room held potential for such fascination in its light form. They might seduce observers by
arousing their curiosity, by intriguing them with a light surplus of wonder. They might even make them want to touch. Maud noticed these initial clues of a teenager's budding affinities, and she oriented her work
thanks to them. The diversity of scattered objects increased the chances
for these connections. And those 'well achieved' but still attainable items
were better candidates for curiosity trials. I saw in these trials a singular technique which attempted to arouse curiosity through specific arrangements of objects and engagements with them. These material dis-
positions amplified their capacity to intrigue.

Figure 11: The three paintings: two in the corner and one above the fireplace.

The curiosity trials carved a middle path in a specific manner. They incorporated modest valorization of artworks and other objects; the acts of pointing to them; sparks of attention from a teenager; and the caregiver's refined abilities to notice the advent of a participant's involvement at the slightest degree. In the case of clowning in dementia care, Hendricks calls this ability to notice the emergence of someone else's curiosity thanks to material things and bodily attitudes the "tackling of indifference" (2012: 459). As I recognized in Maud's technique, this ability was enabled through refined capacities "to distinguish with increasing subtlety between differences in how the other person relates to the world, attentively, physically, and sensorily" (ibid: 469).

Next, Maud told me about a second way to support teens' involvement in the session, by "walking the path". Since La Porte Bleue was set apart from the center, its team went to pick up the teens in the living room. They then walked for five minutes to the other building with them.

"This walk is essential", insisted Maud, "because it allows us to feel the dynamic, what's going on, who has difficulty, who is overloaded, and, maybe, why". With this feeling of that momentary dynamic, she could adjust the start of the session, as she described when pointing to a sentence on a blackboard: "For instance, when I wrote this note 'What do we do with all we have in our heads?', it was because I felt on the path that the teens were parasitized with 30.000 questions". Adjusting the session would then equate to finding a better way of involving the teens using their dynamic at that moment. But when moving to the new building, La Porte Bleue was relocated inside it, on the first floor. The team often spoke about the loss of this possibility to "walk the path together". Even though it was a much shorter route, the teachers and caregivers kept coming to join teenagers in the living room. Sometimes they sat on the sofas for a quick chat together before going upstairs. This moment for feeling out the dynamic before entering the proper space of the workshop remained important for adjusting the mood at the start of the session.

Then, once in the rooms, their arrangement should allow one to avoid confrontation within proximity. When everybody came in, Maud told me, they would all come sit around a big central table, with pieces of paper and colored markers available on it. While sitting together, adults included, each participant wrote or drew a 'mood note'. "This is done very quickly", specified Maud, "but it gives an attitude to arriving teens... That we wouldn't be around the table, in a face-to-face confrontation, with nothing to do". From these first moments onwards, the material spaces mattered for organizing each person's presence within the group, thanks to the same layout in both rooms. They presented chairs around a central table, and one or two smaller tables in corners, again, suggested to adjust one's comfortable distance (figure 12). After having gathered around the central table, participants split in one or two rooms depending on whether they were working on schoolwork or a creative project. The rooms were not big. Many displayed objects or storage cabinets closely surrounding the tables. Maud underlined how much, "the space was used everywhere", meaning that it was better to avoid vast open spaces. Proximity safeguarded caregivers against addressing the adolescents in a confrontational way, Maud detailed, just as did their bodily placement towards them: "We should not be too intrusive, so I avoid the face-to-face position. ... I try to position us side-by-side, but not too close either. I place myself a bit angled, like this". In a swift move, she stepped her chair back from mine and turned it a bit aslant (figure 13). "Sometimes, we should come nearer because we put our attention on the mediating object, not on the person. But still, the gaze should not be too threatening".

Gathering to write quick notes before spreading, or spacing ones' body aslant within proximity; these two tricks worked with a spatial organization of presences. This spatial organization enabled participants to elude the face-to-face confrontations that risked hindering their involvement in a learning task. This organization manifested a strong contrast with the layout of traditional classrooms, where each person sits behind a single table, facing the board and teacher at a relative distance. It became plain, with the move to the new building, that this contrast was in no way modifiable. While the architects had first designed La Porte Bleue as a small classroom with an annex, caregivers made clear that this setting was not an option at all. So the two adjacent rooms went back to being conceived as small workshop spaces, with storage furniture, central tables, and others in corners (figures 14a-b).

Figure 12: Map of La Porte Bleue before the move, in the separate house.

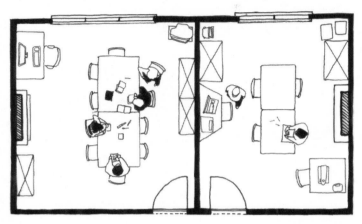

Figure 13: The caregiver's body placement in proximity, avoiding a confrontational position.

Figure 14a: Architects' plan of La Porte Bleue (14/10/13), firstly designed as a small classroom. Courtesy of Pierre Lenders & Antoinette Defay.

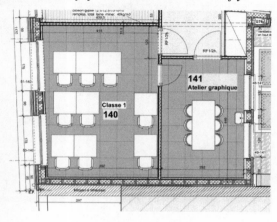

Figure 14b: Architects' plan as built (09/04/14), now designed as two workshop rooms with storage furniture. Courtesy of Pierre Lenders & Antoinette Defay.

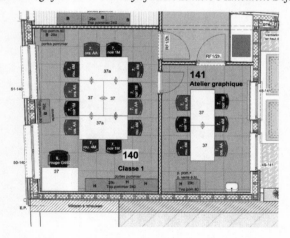

A last spatial trait that I denoted in Maud's account was her singular usage of the two rooms. In both the former house and the new building, artistic activities were separated from individual schoolwork in an adjacent room. Maud "juggled" with both rooms, she said abruptly. Before I could interrupt her with a question, she went on:

> That's an extremely important hook, the plastic art, for all the young people who are in need of learning, because we can juggle. For example, when schoolwork turns difficult, one can take a break and go there to make a small basket. We use plastic art because it is so rewarding to make and finalize projects. ... Here [in the schoolwork room], it doesn't work anymore?! Ok, let's go next door! The art workshop brings a slight diversion of things and it supports [participants]. It helps to return to the project with a crooked path, with self-satisfaction, with a finished product that one is proud of and comes to show back here. Because, at the end of each session, we all return to the central table [to tell what they've done].
>
> I interjected: And how do you that, juggling?
>
> She replied: Well, I avoid any reaction like 'ah no, that's not good any longer!' And sometimes you want to do it, to say 'Hey, come on, that's enough!' But I try not to let it get until that point of tension. So I'm very quick to pay attention to what's not working well ... We should stay in a serene environment as most as possible for that. It doesn't mean that we erase all the problems, but that we're going to be as close as possible to what's actually happening... So that things don't come to damage youth's relationship to learning as well as our goals.

Juggling the rooms required an acute attentiveness for noticing very quickly when a blockage occurred with a youth. It required reacting before the school difficulty bogged them down, and before tensions needed to be addressed in an educational way. Teenagers' involvement in their learning activity was sustained with this particular adjustment of quick noticing within a close space and juggling different rooms, with different purposes.

Along the interview with Maud I better perceived how the spaces, together with caregivers' use of them, facilitated teens' involvement. They

displayed objects in an attempt to raise curiosity. They walked paths together to better feel a momentary dynamic. Caregivers also spaced their
body within proximate interactions. Or they juggled with rooms as soon
as a blockage peeped out. Caregivers' adjustments thanks to these spatial arrangements were core to further enabling the teens' involvement
in learning tasks. Importantly, the team of La Porte Bleue insisted, these
adjustments would hardly be possible with the setting of a school and its
classrooms. Classrooms are traditionally embedded with the themes of
order and discipline (Markus 1993: 41–94). The details of their equipment
are designed for framing the conditions in which pupils are supposed
to learn. When allocated to their seats in rows, pupils' bodies are static.
Their gazes are turned towards a raised platform, from which the teacher
addresses all of them simultaneously. This strongly framed setting keeps
out, in recreation areas and corridors, possibilities to venture into unexpected encounters among many different movements. The spaces of
the pedagogical workshop diverged from that traditional, but still very
common setting of the classroom. This was due to the slight messiness of
things, the path to be walked together in random motions, the organization of presences, non-confrontational ways of addressing, and the adjacent creative room. I'm not saying that such crammed and more loosely
structured rooms were better than classrooms in general. But their contrasts, and maybe also other ones, were essential for aiding unsettled
teenagers to get involved again in learning. Mingling pedagogic and care
practices requires such an alternative frame and the tactful adjustments
it enables.

Sensing a specific world

Except for the pedagogic workshop, activities existed neither for the purpose of learning skills, nor were teenagers supposed to continue these
activities after their stay. They were not expected to become experts in
making mosaics or writing poetry. It was their involvement in the moment that mattered, however inelegantly it happened. During my first
few months, it also became clear that providing material conditions to

catch on participants in the moment could hardly happen without appealing to their bodily senses. And this, for each workshop, was set up in a highly specific manner.

The episode with Sandro was particularly telling on this point. One morning, while seven teens were leaving for the clay workshop, Sandro did not move at all. I had gotten to know Sandro two days earlier at the painting workshop, where I had confronted him about his sexual jokes towards a younger girl. We had enjoyed a chat, too, about painted ceramic tilework called *azulejos*. Sandro knew them well due to his Portuguese origin. I sat next to him. He did not want to go to the clay workshop because, he muttered to me, due to the little sleep he had had last night, he knew that he would easily be carried away by the group agitation, and things would go awry. I asked him if he had already gone to the clay workshop. "No". "Me neither", I replied, and added that I'd been told about the studio several times due to its very special atmosphere, outside the center. The external and particular location intrigued him a bit. So I went on giving him an idea of what modeling clay was like. I tried to awaken his curiosity with concrete evocations and links between the craftwork of clay and tiles. He agreed to try it out. We then walked out of the building, passed a few houses, and turned onto the path of one of them. We crossed a longish, leafy garden, and headed towards a small brick house at the rear (figure 15). Sandro was surprised to discover this environment, quite distinct from the center.

Entering the small house brought more discoveries. Its interior spatial layout interlaced different areas, with a central table and several side tables in nooks and crannies. More than a corner suggesting distance adjustments, this whole convoluted organization of compartments, caregivers commented later, was arranged to avoid the ordering typical of factories. Indeed, the spatial organization of the atelier circumvented the factory logic of parceling out spaces and people into hierarchical leadership, functional tasks, and interchangeable workers (Bouchy 1981). The compartments eluded the technical and depersonalized organization of spaces that work with a division of tasks and gestures in stiffened chronometric cadences. When we entered, Alix, a ceramist, greeted us with aprons and asked where we wanted to sit. Many teens were already at the central table. Remembering Sandro's expectation of getting involved in the bustle of the group due to his lack of sleep, I proposed to him that we sit at a table off to the side. Convolution enables such flexibility for irregular placements and, as we'll see, unexpected moves along the way.

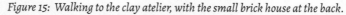

Figure 15: Walking to the clay atelier, with the small brick house at the back.

Another prominent trait of the clay atelier was intriguing. Compartments held arrays of objects that gave clues about the process of crafting: here, long shelves with dozens of clay sculptures, there, others with pots full of colored pigments, or still manual tools in wood or metal, artworks in the making, an oven, and a pallet full of clay packets in another corner (figure 16). As with the displayed objects in La Porte Bleue, these unusual things were good candidates for tickling curiosity. But here, the coherence between these objects added something else. As much as the small brick house and its location at the back of a garden, the collection of these specific objects featured the clay atelier as a small world apart from the center. Indeed, like the compact discs that music lovers used to amass on shelves, valuing appreciations in practice also leans on material arrangements as they organize specific worlds, with their own tools, aesthetic styles and (temporary) boundaries, offering ways to contemplate or handle these objects (Hennion, Gomart & Maisonneuve 2000: 218–219).

Figure 16: The objects and compartments of the atelier.

While Sandro and I settled with the things we'd need, we passed by sculptures of elephants displayed on a window ledge, and started to model pieces off that inspiration. Touching and manipulating the clay increasingly infused the material with more specificity. Sculpting the design involved working the clay until it softened in the heat of our hands. It involved soft pushes on the dough with our fingertips, flattening it a bit more here, creating a depression there, holding the piece at different angles. We formed different shapes, trying to homogenize their surfaces as best as we could. With the help of tools way sharper than our fingers, we dug, removed, and displaced mass. We curved corners until we rounded their edges. Though the body-object contact mostly passed by the hands, it was also moderated by our aprons which hoarded traces of dirt. Manipulating the clay brought us into intimate contact with it.[5] Where spatial convolution enabled irregular seating, the craftwork with its tactile sensibility invited personal interactions with the clay and tools.[6] And so we kept smoothing out here, and smoothing out there, until, before the end of the session, Sandro got visibly tired and could not focus anymore. We then passed by the shelves and had a closer look at the many sculptures. Other care centers belonging to this institution also used the atelier, and the collection of artworks was impressive. The numerous handicrafts displayed a diversity of figures and textures. Like our pieces, every sculpture was infused with the unique specificity of a personal creation. The specificity of the clay atelier did not only belong to the type of activity in itself. That atelier also gained singularity when the accumulation of artworks reshaped its specific features.

---

5   These manipulations echo Sennett's (2008) study about craft culture. He argues that objects become interesting through the development of a "material consciousness" (120). That is, not a consciousness independent from things, but the particular forms of awareness that come throughout the work done with and to a thing we can change (ibid: 119–146).

6   In her history of tactile sensations, Classen (2012: 167–197) recounts how modern institutions set up from the 19th century, like schools, prisons or armies, trained inmates to socially conform through the standardization of movements, leaving few margins for personal touches or idiosyncratic behavior. In schools (although a few students always kept displaying eccentric manners) these uniform bodies were intended to increase the efficiency and productivity of future laborers. Here it seems that what is sought is the opposite of routine discipline: the craftwork fosters an expansion of personal traits, within a setting that exhibits these singular artworks, and draws participants in compelling manipulations without imposing gestural patterns.

The clay atelier made tangible how much each workshop setting, even those that did not involve the creation of artifacts, featured a specific world that appealed to bodily senses in its own way. Touch might not always be the most prominent one, although it was often solicited, whether in gardening, cooking, or assembling mosaics. Watching a movie or playing music obviously emphasized visual and auditory attention, whereas walking through the city or dancing was very much about bodily movements. Each of these corporal practices implied specific sensory richness, and each of their material framing organized a world that called to those senses.

Side slippages

Then, of course, it also happened that teens' involvement in a workshop failed. When activities took place outside, especially, their conditions were more friable, more porous to unexpected temptations. Hearing caregivers' accounts of outside activities, it stood out how much a group departure or traveling defied stability not only in the moment, but at the venue thereafter. The teens' involvement was easily sidetracked, sometimes precipitating a complete collapse of the activity, and hence put a strain on the care relationship.

Sport fields tended to make the activity drift, maybe because the energetic games worked with rigorous directional cues and stirred the players' excitement. One Friday, we took a tram to reach an indoor football field. Benches for supporters stood along the field, a few meters from the pitch. Like in most sports venues, the fields were coupled with side layouts either for spectators or for the players to rest. Joachim, a fifteen-year-old, did not take part in the game. As I was not taking part either, we both sat on these benches, where he quickly started a chat. He told me about video games, his favorite occupation to which he devotes most of his time, before asking what I do with my spare time. My answer plunged us into a one-hour conversation. We completely forgot about the match, barely arching an eyebrow at occasional interpersonal clashes. Joachim seemed to enjoy it. And so did I. The next Monday morning, in the team meeting, Baptiste reported on how the sport outing had gone, and turned towards me: "Joachim and you stayed on the side. I didn't come closer to you both, because I felt that something was happening. Would you like to say something about it?" To my surprise, this sideline, informal, and unexpected chat was worth being related to the team. Apparently, such side involvements next to the planned activity were as important for the care work. It required me to immediately sort out what I would relate to the team or not, in order to respect the privacy of the chat I had with Joachim. The football field with its lines on the floor and goals regulated and qualified how teens should move or throw the ball to each other. But these lines also delimited side spaces that offered opportunities for other involvements. Hence crafting other bubbles, like an informal conversation, was part of the whole activity that fed caregivers' exchanges. The teens might want to follow another track, and these deviations gave more possibilities for caregivers to know them and work with them.

Well, this was the case insofar this other track did not threaten the main activity. Venturing outside more likely risked unexpected disturbances, and these disinvolvements could turn the activity upside down. The following week, Baptiste related an outing dedicated to badminton. According to him, it completely failed, starting with the challenge of the departure:

> It was such a complicated session. Already when leaving, Emil was glad to have the whole panoply of his sportswear, but then he had forgotten his shorts at home. On the traveling: no problem. But once we arrived on the spot, the hall was busy with a group of young ladies. So David and Aymane started to observe them. We told them ten or so times that we would stay in the cloakroom until everybody was ready and the girls had finished. But it was extremely complicated. Aymane went out all the time, so we had to go to find him. After, on the field, compared to last week, when we had a possibility to play with teens, where we could really be into a sort of exchange between us, this time it was not possible. I think we couldn't end any match. And I also think it's now three times that they have gone there and they are starting to

be fed up with it. So it was extremely hard. Eduardo then followed and did at least thirty times his joke, when he taps someone's shoulder and then hides. And he really did it *thir-ty-times* [he emphasized]. Thus, I had to tell him thirty times that it was not the right time and place to do that. [...] So when we came back here, we gathered them again in the resting room. [...] It was odd because some of them seemed to say they had a great afternoon: Lucien, Aymane, and Eduardo—he has his good reasons. They said the bad atmosphere was due to us [Baptiste and the other caregiver] because we didn't stop reminding everyone of the framework. But then, it was extremely tiresome. I told them that in these conditions, it was difficult to go outside with them.

Baptiste reported the failed activity as a cascading effect: the derailed departure, then the girls were a distraction, and this mess drove Eduardo in his diversion with his above-average sense of humor. To the caregivers, the activity failed not only because it was not possible to play. It especially failed because they simply could not share the activity with the adolescents. While doing activities together, caregivers were always reluctant to formalize their relationship with them. Recalling the framework of the activity turned their relationship into an educational one. However, to the teens, the afternoon had been great. They had had a lot of fun running after girls and making jokes. Again, their disinvolvement was part of the care work. It led Baptiste to discuss it with them afterwards in the resting room. And the teens' responses made him wonder if they were 'fed up' with that activity, impelling him to propose another one to better sustain their interest over time (I explore this issue in the next chapter). Even though outings opened up more opportunities to slippages away from the main activity, venturing outside remained central to continuing to work with the adolescents and their unexpected responses to activities. Whether a single teen 'misses the boat' and stays away, or several of them completely ruin a session, these disinvolvements did matter for care work. They could carve new relational tracks (as with Joachim), risk turning caregivers' relationship to teenagers into a corrective one, or provoke the team's interrogation of teens' interests.

Passages

The involvement of adolescents took many forms along the workshops I attended or heard about, day after day. Perhaps you feel slightly dizzy at this point, after having been given a taste of these various venues, each evoking a different set of specificities. To be precise, each workshop showed yet another way through which their spatial arrangements were to provide conditions for luring participants into a particular activity. Reaching a state of concentration was set up very differently when watching a movie or writing, as well as when switching from these respective forms of attention towards group exchanges. Other activities, like going to the cinema, demanded a minimal framing. They relied more on a practical framework than on a material setting, simply encouraging teens' reflexivity on what they were doing. Overall, the spatial conditions of workshops weren't suggestive like the ambiguous possibilities of the living spaces. What is supposed to be done in an atelier or on a sport field is unequivocal, even if their disposition often leaves margins for each participant to respond in the way they tend to. Think of Karl who, both in the radio and cooking workshops, threw himself into technical tasks but ignored opportunities for spontaneous interaction. Or remember the clay atelier that involved us personally in tactile sensations, inspired by singular handicrafts on shelves, while its layout enabled flexibility for irregular placements.

If each workshop venue and its practical framework are a set of specificities, then I can draw few common traits among them. Except, perhaps, that they are all about easing the passage from one state to another. Law and Moser (1999) argue that being or not being able to do something is, in practice, a matter of good or bad passages between different sets of specificities. A passage can be understood in a material sense, like when the woman in a wheelchair they interview can't board a train because there's no hoist that connects it to the platform. The movement between specific settings, they write, is a set of specificities as well. A passage isn't only material, but also transformative: thanks to a setting, like a hoist, one becomes able to do something that wasn't possible without it. When achieving or falling short of personal goals, the authors continue, all of us make and are made by good or bad passages.

What else were workshop spaces and caregivers doing than creating such passages? I mean, not only material passages (although walks were sometimes included), but transformative passages: the transitions that increased the chances to drive teens into their relational affinities.[7] A transformative passage would occur, for instance, when they engrossed or switched their attention, became more curious about something, or experienced, felt, tested bodily movements and senses. I say "increased the chances", because teens' involvement remained an uncertain and unstable form of attachment. They were uncertain because they always happened on a middle path, between a person, things, and other possible mediators. And they were unstable because at any moment they could fade out due to fatigue, conflicts, or distractions on the spot, to name only a few potential roadblocks. These passages show that teens involvement is a form of attachment that comes into existence while remaining on the verge of fading.

Some passages that seem easy in fact prove difficult, like when Jimmy reflected on the duration of screening and called for a revision of the framework. And some passages that initially seem difficult are eventually made easier, for instance, thanks to specific sensory appeals. When facing schoolwork, the curiosity trials and Maud's other adjustments with the spaces of the pedagogical workshop facilitated the teens' passage from apprehension to learning activities. A passage that fails can have good or bad consequences for the care work, or both. Teens'

---

7   More dimensions are at stake in such a passage than simply shifting from one state to another. Hennion, Gomart and Maisonneuve (2000: 188–204) identify that a passionate state emerges through different forms of passage: swaying between bodily feelings and mind intentions; successful meetings between individual actions and socio-technical apparatuses; shifts from active preparation to being passively caught by a sensation; and passages from technical commands to uncontrollable occurrences. Though the passages I emphasize here mean the transformation of someone' state rather than their traveling, they are significantly different from the 'rites of passage', dear to anthropologists, whose ceremony marks a milestone or major change in someone's life.

disinvolvement on the sport field opened up the team's reflection on their loss of interest, but also compelled the purely educational relationship from which caregivers wanted to escape as much as possible. In any case, these passages from one state to another, in and out of involvement, oscillating between indifference and a more intense contact, never merely occupied the teens' days. Not a single day flew by without the caregivers reiterating the importance of these passages as they related them. In doing so, they kept deepening their knowledge of each teens' motivations, sensibilities, current difficulties and abilities. And so they kept adjusting their care work according to that informal knowledge, shaped and reshaped by the responses from the adolescents.

Chapter 4
Variations of interest, variations of space

Over the year, something else became visible: these material spaces did not stay the same. The photographs below render it clearly. They show the marks of eight months on the yard (figures 17a-b). During that time, the ping-pong table lost its central position, the fresco on the wall was repainted, benches were built with a wooden pallet, and more vegetation was planted. Apparently, caregivers together with the teens made the material spaces vary. But why and how did they do that? When I asked Baptiste about these spatial variations, he linked the workshops to the problem of boredom. He described it as follows:

> There comes a moment [when] we need to nourish again. Workshops really need to adapt, either because we [caregivers] are bored, or because the youth's group dynamic, who is there at that time, doesn't lend itself to a particular set-up of the activity. So it needs to adapt to the group and to our interest, that is, always keeping [caregivers'] curiosity regarding what we do for our care work. If we do the same thing again [and again], it is not interesting. So a break [from a workshop] is necessary for nourishing again, and for creating the willingness to resume it later.

The caregivers' interest in workshops and the teens' group dynamics had temporalities. At some point, variations were crucial for their interest not to fade into boredom. As in the previous chapter, with the badminton outing that failed, the team often questioned whether the teens were 'fed up' with an activity, causing their disinvolvement. But caregivers also needed to maintain their own curiosity in what they were doing. It was necessary for them to turn towards new activities, or boredom risked impoverishing the care work. On one hand, Baptiste further nuanced, boredom was welcome within the frame of an activity, since these "floating moments" would "leave opportunities for teenagers to seize it [to do something with it]". This nuance recalls the framing of uncertain involvement in the previous chapter. But on the other hand, boredom was a problem in the long run, because, he added: "if the caregiver does not carry the wish for the workshop [anymore], the participants won't be wanting [to do it] after a while, if not from the outset." In short, the caregivers' lasting interest in the activities they led was a vital support for participants' involvement. Whereas in the previous chapters, I noted that participants' familiarity with living spaces or involvement in an activity emerged out of indifference, here a lasting interest had to forestall boredom over time. No interest could survive without variation, just as always eating the same meal would make you lose your appetite.

Figures 17a: The yard of the old townhouse in June 2013.

Figure 17b: The yard of the old townhouse in March 2014.

In this chapter I take up the challenge of exploring how variations of material spaces relate to the revival of interest. Teens' and caregivers' interest is a form of attachment that extended my research focus, from the very moments when their sensations manifested together through their engagements with objects, towards the collective of people and equipment that allowed their tastes to change over time, along with their evanescence and revival (Hennion, Gomart & Maisonneuve 2000: 143–145). The stories I assemble below cover longer periods of time compared to the daily scenes of interactions I have described so far. With these stories I examine how the team and the adolescents succeeded or failed to maintain their interest in activities, through several strategies aiming at enrolling one another in affinities current to the group. I recognize such strategies of enrollment in the hybrid arrangements of the building, in caregivers' exchanges about daily events, in their discussions with teens during community meetings or in their subsequent adjustments of chosen activities, and their interest also varied in a less formal manner in what we called 'waves'. By scrutinizing different spatial variations, it will come into view that sustaining interest often relies on slight, furtive forms of attachment, such as familiarity with the teens or their involvement in a moment. The smallest of these attachments nourished the care work: every little teen affinity could count for caregivers, no matter how small. It turned out, too, that sustaining interest could increase the importance of these modest affinities to the point of materializing them in the institutional place, keeping this place attuned to what currently mattered within the group.

A pragmatic view of interest

As I continued to ask questions about spatial variations, several caregivers emphasized how much they took shape between their interests and that of the teens. Berenice articulated it this way:

> We need to take pleasure in workshops because, if you do a workshop that you cannot carry with enough pleasure, then it doesn't work [teens do not get involved in it]. [...] Meanwhile it is important to consider how we readapt it to teens. So it should meet the team's and the teenagers' interest. For instance, if one group of teens says there are not enough sports, then we can add some. And at the same time, some workshops always remain. ... But, yes, for sure, that means that the spaces will vary accordingly!

A 'variation' was not just about caregivers' and teens' individual pleasure in the moment. Rather, a variation germinated with the emergence of an interest between certain caregivers, teenagers, and an ongoing or potential activity. Such an understanding meets a pragmatic view on 'interest'. Dewey (1983 [1916]; 2011 [1939]: 93) argues that an interest does not pre-exist "in" an individual or a group, but it develops as a relation between people and their aims, and encompasses the means for connecting them. An interest is not static, nor it is reduced to a psychological concern, but it's a practical, enduring activity that can also chafe against obstacles.

Remember Kevin who, at some point, despite the considerable deepening of his interest in care for animals, eventually ran away to roam the city. He was carried along by other aspirations, and by other means on which the team had little grip. But in their practice, the caregivers used particular mediations that allowed me to look, as Dewey proposes, at the concrete means and obstacles that contribute to the social process of realizing interests. Such interests are redefined in interaction with others, who then become involved. In this way, interest can progressively lead to a renewed situation.

In the day center, one such means for the collective realization of interests was a chart of the weekly program of activities. It was a big polystyrene panel, with movable activity labels fastened with bits of Velcro, and it stood on the mantle of a fireplace, right in the middle of the caregivers' office (figure 18). On its left side, the panel included about twenty workshops that had been previously done. They constituted a sort of reserve of activities that had proved to be of interest but were currently not planned. This side column was then an intermediary space for interests that came and went. Each year, in early September, the team held a meeting to revise the schedule. But the labels danced on that polystyrene panel during the year as well, passing back and forth across its columns, and in and out of the panel, depending whether they were of interest or not during a period of time. Each week, Berenice used the panel to adapt the program and she completed it with more details on a Word document. She then reprinted it and posted it on the door of the office, to make it easy to glance at. The chart enabled all to visualize the growth and demise of interests shared in the day center over time. It pointed to more unpredictable flows of appreciation that could come along the year, making one wonder how this would occur.

But Berenice mentioned another feature of interest. Some activities were permanent. They remained interesting on a stable basis. These everlasting interests in unchanging activities were indeed visible in caregivers' annual reports.[1] Amid the bunches of renewed activities that popped up every few years, some of them didn't change. Yet they

---

1   I analyzed these reports back to eight years prior to my arrival.

were able to be modified when needed. Horse riding was one of the activities that never fell out of fashion. Marion, the accompanying caregiver, reported numerous therapeutic aspects that manifested during sessions. She described how teens ventured into new bodily sensations, or wove special relationships with the horses. Year after year, several teens were always keen to sign up for it. But questions arose along the way. It happened, for instance, that Marion wondered about the strict framework required by riding instructors at the farm. Instructors didn't know about teens' particular troubles, which Marion saw as a good thing in a readaptation context. But at some point, the adolescents manifested a need for more flexibility towards them and their difficulties. Marion then adapted the framework by establishing a talking time at the end of each session, so that participants could express what they had gone through, and share it with the instructors. Thus, even with activities sufficiently interesting to secure a lingering spot in the weekly program, internal adaptations occurred throughout their realization.

Despite the permanence of certain activities, in this chapter my challenge is to understand how workshop modifications could grow big enough to bring about spatial changes. In order to maintain interest over time, caregivers and teens reoriented their approach towards new activities. For this, they followed particular processes. Callon and Law's (1982) examination of how interests take shape in scientists' practice is particularly helpful here. An interest may succeed or fail, they write, through "strategies of enrollment" (619), that is, specific processes of seeking out the interests of others, of attempting to make something of value to them. The submission of a paper to a scientific journal entails such strategies of enrollment, like when the content of the first paragraph illustrates a wider issue with a specific one. When scientists explore which journal to target, they too assess how each would better catch and transform readers' interests. Unfortunately, this transformation may not succeed. The editors may reject the paper, or they may give feedback that proposes to transform the authors' interest. An 'enrollment', then, denotes the actions and ruses through which a role is attributed to someone else who will accept it, if they become interested,

and these attempts can be reciprocal.[2] The notion of 'strategies of enrollment' refines my pragmatic view of interest: it enables a closer look
into the variations I encountered in the day center, because it points to
strategies operated in the aim of forming an interest that is liable to
change. More than the social and practical processes Dewey signals, this
approach to the transformation of interests is "precisely about how it is
that the small become big (or vice versa), and why it is that some succeed
while others fail" (ibid: 621). It thus points, too, to the constitution of
certain social and material worlds, and to the dissolution of others.
So what were the strategies of enrollment in the day center? How did
caregivers' and teens' interests transform? And how did the variations
of material spaces relate to these revivals of interest?

*Figure 18: A tool for revisions during the year: the flexible chart on a polystyrene
panel.*

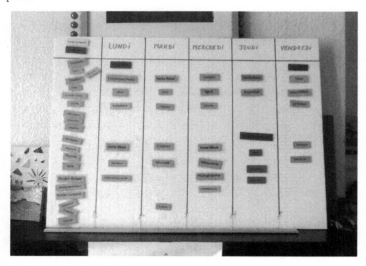

---

2   About this understanding of 'interest' as a translation process (or, roughly said,
     as an ensemble of relationships that entail the transformation of a social and
     natural world), see also Callon's (1986) famous analysis of the controversy about
     the decline in the population of scallops in St. Brieuc Bay.

Hybrid buildings

There was, of course, one tangible means that I could hardly ignore when looking for enrollment in shared interests: the buildings. Not the edifices of the old house or the new one in themselves, but that both were hybrid. The day just before the official inauguration, I came across two cleaning ladies hired by an external company. After having spent two days cleaning the whole new building, they could not help wondering, they told me with a mix of confusion and curiosity, "what is this building?! What is this institution that contacted our company? What do they do?" No typology of building they knew was recognizable in that hybrid structure. It is not a home, but its living spaces are central. It is not a cultural center, but it has workshop rooms of all sorts. It is not a school, but two of its rooms serve the atypical pedagogic setting of La Porte Bleue. It is not a hospital, but it has a nursery and consultation rooms. It is not a park, but it has a big garden with two benches, each flanked by a waste bin. But it is an institution, indeed; it has a secretary desk, waiting seats at the entrance, and several corridors. The cleaning ladies' wondering about the building brought to mind other newcomers' astonishment about its unusual and unidentifiable aspect, whether they were teenagers, new trainees or caregivers, delivery workers, or other external visitors. These buildings were typologically hybrid. This way, they avoided becoming spaces with conventional purpose. They worked with patches of different arrangements for situations that usually occur in different places.

But the thing was, the hybrid typology of these buildings didn't suffice to make room for variations of interest within the group. In a meeting for preparing the resettlement, while caregivers bent over the architects' plans and examined the rooms for distributing activities, several voices reminded that, anyway, the rooms should "remain open to change". This request didn't frighten the architects. From the start of the collaboration, they had been told that the team worked with ongoing questioning. Since the architects wished to equip the care center as best as possible, they accepted to leave the building partially undefined. Their strategy was to design rooms of diverse size, shape, light, acoustics, texture, and withdrawn or centrally located space. This diversity could make this or that room better suitable to try in this or that workshop. More-over, when the group settled in, they dispersed tools or materials among these spots, without strictly delineating a unique purpose for each of them. Rather, the different spots of the hybrid building were permeated with objects drawing fuzzy boundaries about the kind of activity that might be done here or there. The team gave these spots some vague names, too, offering clues about an imprecise ensemble of activities, like 'sport', 'creation', 'relaxation', 'media', etc. The rooms' diversity of shapes, together with their imprecise boundaries due to their contents and names, left them open to later variations by offering a diversity of options for setting up a workshop. The partially undefined building would then become even more hybrid according to new interests that would emerge over the course of the practice.

From there, a variation might be of very different scale, from small to more consequent interventions, and it might enroll more or fewer people and means. Note the following contrast between two workshops, both stemming from community meetings with teens. One aimed to explore the theme of 'adulthood' and was barely defined at its start. The first sessions would take form as meetings with all participants. They would browse through different themes about becoming adults, then decide on outings or other activities to engage with this topic. When caregivers discussed where to do that workshop, they looked for a 'convivial setting' that might help to cultivate interest in exchanges while making these meetings pleasurable moments. Caregivers first thought to do it in the living spaces, but these ones too easily led teens to "collapse on the couches" or to turn towards other potentially distracting opportunities. Instead they needed something more formal, but still providing pleasure. After considering several options, they decided that the bright room of the first floor would work – the room that was also chosen for the writing atelier in chapter three. Its central table would host the meeting, and the computers on the side could eventually be used for a little research. But it would work, with a small variation of bringing in a tray with a teapot, cups, and cookies, placed in the middle of the table.[3]

In contrast, a gardening workshop drove far more consequences and spatial rearrangements. One morning, Louis, a technical worker of the institution, was assembling a shed in a corner on the terrace of the new building. On the other side of the garden, Sylvie, a caregiver, was weeding. When I approached her to ask about this gardening activity, she branched her answer out into a wealth of stories. It started with these flowers planted by an official gardener to make the place 'nice' for the inauguration. She strongly disliked these exotic ornamentals. So she discreetly pulled them out, she said to me in a slight laugh, and replaced them with the kind of flowers she liked. Meanwhile, this lured some teens to join her. They decided together to seed some vegetables that then grew, and Josie cooked them. But Sylvie needed to learn more skills for furthering that workshop, for better grounding the adolescents' interest. With another caregiver, they went to a one-day training in vegetable gardening. At that time, by chance they learned that Sami, the head of the institution's technical workers, was passionate about gardening and knew a lot about it. Since then, as soon as they had a question, they would call him. He, too, became committed to improving that spot and growing veggies. To Sylvie, every element in these stories counted. Especially since teens' interest in that garden was fluctuating over time, some new tools, the seeds, a shed, skills, Sami's advice, or Josie's cooking; all were necessary to keep it alive. Whereas a variation might suffice by enhancing a table with a tea set, here it gathered many ingredients that nourished participants' interest, along which the garden varied with its flowers, vegetables, sheds and equipment.

Departing from the partially undefined building, a variation could involve a bunch of social and material transformations, or minimal ones.

---

3   Such minimal interventions in spatial arrangements for heightening pleasure closely echoes Vogel and Mol (2014). They recount from the weight consultants they interviewed how material surroundings could contribute to cultivate pleasure in eating, as it would not be distracting (for instance with media) but attractive (as with a nicely set table).

It could enroll more or less people, means, and money. The aim was to create the right conditions for keeping caregivers and teens interested in their daily activities. Whatever its size, each variation increased the hybrid, unconventional aspect of the building, making it more specific to the appreciations and concerns that took shape within the group over time.

Intriguing daily events

But then, the strategy adopted in the arrangements and uses of the building left a blind spot: how did caregivers and teens translate their ideas or first-hand experiences into greater, broader interests? Meetings, to which I turn now, were a central means for that process. In the previous chapters I described how caregivers related everyday stories during their staff meetings, continually reshaping an informal knowledge about each adolescent, their familiar bonds, involvement in activities, and surprising changes, however piecemeal. Now I want to emphasize another path in which these daily exchanges resulted. The small, seemingly insignificant occurrences that caregivers related in meetings and daily chats were a fertile ground, too, for a growing revival of interest.

This became clear with the story of the staff's new resting room. In the new building, this room was designed as a 'break room' for the team. It catered to norms about workers' need for breaks during the day. But its location away from the living spaces, common office, and nearby hotspots posed a problem. The caregivers had to cross a corridor and go to an upper floor to reach it. So they did not go there. It was, they explained to me, "too disconnected from the life of the center", which was "not the way we work… At least, not for now". From what exactly did they refuse to disconnect when being away from the "life of the center"? Sylvie specified, "[The caregivers' office] is a crossing point where information circulates and we catch it. And if you're not there, you don't have the information. Well, you'll have it later in a meeting, but it's not the same." And she added, with a playful smile, "you don't have the anecdote, you don't have the little gems." Sylvie pointed to an ongoing mode of communication in the care practice. When caregivers passed by in their office, they used to tell each other about situations that had just happened with the youths. These anecdotes enabled them to share much more interesting stories with colleagues, compared to the synthetic versions communicated in meetings, because fresh anecdotes led to spontaneous advice on how to improvise a right response to a youth and to their state of the day.

The staff break room foregrounded how much caregivers' closeness to daily events in the center mattered, and enabled them to work by discussing occurrences they'd just noticed. In chapter two, I wrote of the surprising minor changes to the familiar portrait that caregivers came to associate with each teen. I wrote of Safia's unusual attitude that contrasted with her earlier stillness. One of the unusual things she did was to take a dance step to one side as she encountered her image in a mirror. When she did it again another day, Berenice was around, who then started to do it with her. It turned into a funny moment that Berenice related during the next morning meeting: "I was behind, mimicking her movements and sometimes asked her to change to another move. [...] It was so funny! I don't know what she had that day, but she was in a good shape! And fun, fun, really full of humor". The dance step story sparked interest among the staff, especially since Safia had barely started to engage outside of her quiet routines. The team then spoke about resuming a hip-hop dance workshop. A trainee was sufficiently skilled to lead it. They scanned some facilities where they might find a room. The idea was launched; they now had to test it. So the caregivers cultivated an interest by being around the adolescents in a familiar place, and by relating small but surprising occurrences to the team.

In workshops, too, caregivers identified potentially interesting events. A memorable one happened when the group of La Porte Bleue went out to a circus school. The next day, Maud reported that the teens had wrapped themselves in fabrics that hung from wooden beams. Her account captivated the team. "It was like a bodily constraint", she said, "but an interesting one". Her interlocutors fell silent. She pursued:

> With those fabrics, you can go up, put yourself inside, and it swings a
> bit because it is hanging. It's really like a cocoon... And this has such
> an effect! There is such a silence during these moments. The calming
> effect it may create is just astonishing. ... And Martin loves this thing.
> And this is lasting – I mean, it's not for three minutes. He stays in it.
> Ingrid asked: And Kevin did it too?!

Her surprise was shared among the caregivers. They all knew too well
that Kevin, who had not yet run away at that time, was most often unable
to be still. Maud answered:

> Yes, but Kevin goes less than Martin, and he stays less long in it. And he
> hangs over it. His arms fall and his leg goes up like this [she throws her
> limbs in several directions]. Well, it's not exactly the same. But Martin,
> he really took to it! He put himself in it, like this, like a restraint, but
> in the good sense of that term.

The effect of the fabric supports intrigued most of the caregivers. The experience had lured in the teens, brought calm or fun according to each of
them. The team then gauged if it might be possible to hang some fabric
supports in a relaxation room of the new building. The teens' involvements with the fabric supports were small occurrences and they happened only a few times, yet even so, they were tasty ingredients for the
caregivers. Of course, their interest was also due to their concern about
the teens' frequent agitation and about bodily constraint, which is a sensitive matter for those who have experienced it in other psychiatric settings. Speculating about possibly good and calming constraints with agitated teens made the story even more interesting to the team. This special concern fostered a possible variation of their practice and to their
material space.

Sometimes, though, the team took cues from other information
than daily events occurring in the living spaces or in workshops. When
presenting a newcomer prior to his arrival, for instance, ideas might
grow. At a meeting, the psychiatrist spoke about Gery, a teenager who
entered the following week. After explaining his troubles, particularly
his learning disorders, he mentioned the boy's keenness on all things

mechanical. Bike repair was his specialty. The second he said that, all faces turned to Eric. All knew of his willingness to bicycle with the teens. Eric smiled back and clarified that he was not exactly a good mechanic. "Well", replied the psychiatrist, "but you could set up a bicycle repair workshop in which Gery would be the expert. I think he needs to be valued in concrete operations like that". That the teen's affinity could hold a therapeutic potential sounded like a good argument. Everyone agreed with the psychiatrist' proposal, which would then be put to the test once Gery was there. It thus happened that caregivers' interest for a new activity found roots in the taste of an adolescent that happened to match theirs, and even promised therapeutic potential.

Yet most of the time, their strategy of enrollment went through their noticing of small, intriguing occurrences in the daily life they shared. The teens' familiarity and their involvement in workshops nourished caregivers' anecdotes and staff meetings with unpredictable occurrences, with appreciations that could intensify in a moment. Here the team did not compare the adolescents' responses in order to better know them.[4] But they shared those daily events by linking them to issues that were of their proper concern or affinity. Caregivers' reports of those occurrences to the rest of the team comprised a strategy of enrollment that triggered the formation of new interests. This strategy gave to those small occurrences the possibility to drive changes in their practice and place.

Expanding zones, drawing boundaries

An important point about staff meetings was that caregivers related their notes about the teens in their shared office, where the latter were absent. The team spoke of moments they had experienced with the adolescents, yet without directly discussing these incidents with them. And, needless to say, teens and caregivers weren't always on the same wavelength.

---

4   See chapter two, 'Workspaces for informal knowledge' and chapter three, 'Relating involvement'.

The weekly community meetings, in contrast, allowed face-to-face ex-changes. Teens and caregivers gathered to express and share all kinds of issues about their institutional life, and to propose ideas of what they would like to do. Caregivers valued new ideas that could alter some es-tablished customs in the facility. It would give, in their words, "a bit of fresh air" to their practice. The community meeting was another strategy of enrollment, through which the range of ideas that could become of in-terest in the group easily expanded. Meanwhile, these meetings also pro-vided a keen taste of which ingredients were not palatable for the team or for the teens. Quite often, during these direct confrontations, the group had to redefine the boundaries of its zones of interest.

How did that happen? Each week, a new sheet of paper was pinned on a cork panel in the living space, on which everyone could list ideas for the next meeting. This piece of paper was a draft agenda that was then completed during the discussion, pinned back onto the panel, and later consigned to a binder.[5] Participants shared all kinds of subjects that concerned the organization of daily community life, often provoking a tense atmosphere among the teens. They regularly mentioned the mate-rial environment, too, in debate about its decoration, damages, or clean-liness. These uneasy moments seemed quite necessary, for they allowed the team's and adolescents' concerns to meet, clash, and be reshuffled.

To caregivers, the point was to do activities that were therapeutically interesting, that is, activities that induced teens to respond to a pro-posal, so that the team could work with these responses. To what extent a proposition should be framed as 'therapeutic' remained under debate within the team, as discussed in chapter three about the framing of min-imal conditions of everyday activities. Caregivers might bring in ideas of their own taste, but always made sure that these proposals concerned the life of the group, like when choosing what to cook for the upcoming Christmas meal. The only limits were money and insurance conditions for risky outings.

---

5   I attended a dozen community meetings. To get a better sense of the issues at stake and their debates, I read about sixty archived reports going back to two years prior to my arrival on the field.

The teens, as far as I discerned, were not concerned by the therapeutic potential of activities. They mostly wanted to have fun, or at least a good time. Video games, sports, listening to music, accessing a punching ball or a computer, or where and when they were allowed to smoke, were rather their concern. As with outings like theme parks, paintball, go karts, or watching horror movies, some activities that they requested were denied, because caregivers deemed they could incite violent attitudes. Baptiste told me, "It's ok if they do it outside [during their time of not being in the center], but then I tell them that for a group of teenagers in psychiatry, it is not something easy to manage, and we would not encourage that".

But the teens also had their boundaries, which were debated in meeting after meeting. It could even happen that these limits launched a boycott. One day Martin, a youth, put an item on the agenda with which most of his fellows agreed: "no community meetings anymore". This was not so surprising to caregivers; for several weeks, few adolescents had brought an issue to the meetings. Most of them had "nothing to say". They asserted that issues in these meetings were just not interesting. Some caregivers recognized that "something had changed" in recent meetings, which they had also noticed spatially: teens and caregivers did not mingle anymore when sitting together, and they paid less attention to whether the 'broken circle' formed by their chairs enabled everyone to see and hear each participant. When facing the teens' stony silence, it was quite clear that the only way Baptiste was ever going to be able to handle the situation was by reawakening their interest. So he returned the teens' statement in the form of a question: "when is an issue interesting or not, to you?" Martin and other participants replied that "interesting stuff" should be of concern to most of the people attending meetings, and not be repeated over time. From there, some pending propositions could be reopened. They checked whether each issue concerned everyone, and whether it varied from previous subjects. The story of that blockage, though, makes plain that the community meeting was a core strategy in directly engaging the teens and in modulating the zones of interest and pace of their variations.

However, the extension of interests within the group and delineation of their boundaries wasn't only at stake during these meetings. The caregivers still had to carry out the actual realization of proposals. This required other strategies of enrollment. Some of the teens' propositions could start on the wrong track for sparking the caregivers' and other participants' interest, and therefore required adjustment along the way. This happened when some of the youths wanted to go visit a cemetery. The accompanying caregivers were at first rather cold about it, in part because other teenagers feared such a visit. But the proposers kept insisting. So caregivers found a compromise by pairing the visit with a storyteller. She used narratives to frame the walk with the theme of death and its possible evocations. It worked quite well, so the storyteller was hired for further visits to other sites to be practiced as storytelling walks. That variation in practice enabled the enrollment of participants who were at first reluctant.

It also happened the other way around, that the accomplishment of a proposition threatened a nascent interest along the way because it proved too demanding and long-lasting. One bunch of teenagers were initially very enthusiastic to improve two rooms where they had been dwelling. Choosing pieces and colors was exciting during the first sessions. But when participants had to keep painting walls and to remain concentrated while doing repetitive technical gestures, they grew weary. Caregivers had to constantly push to keep it going. They eventually achieved the work alone. They still remember having grown remarkably tired of it. The renovation made sense to all the participants, but their interest in the activity was far from easy to sustain from start to finish.

To sum up, the community meetings constituted another means for weaving interest between the team and the adolescents. Whereas in staff meetings, the team related small occurrences, here the strategy of enrollment implied more straightforward investigations that rendered palpable which interests might appeal to other members of the group or not. Face-to-face exchanges with the teens nourished variations of activities and their settings by extending their range, but also by drawing boundaries. Such extensions and boundaries of interest were then reassessed through the realization of the selected activities. A corollary strategy to enroll more participants was to adapt the workshop along the way. But sustaining interest along a workshop completion could also fail, as with the wall painting, leaving the team somewhat wary of doing it again.

Waves

Not every interest was put on trial in staff or community meetings. Though at first it was difficult to decipher how it happened, interests sometimes spread within the group and drove spatial variations much more informally. In interviews with the caregivers and adolescents, I further distinguished a much more discreet strategy of enrollment. We came to call it 'waves'. Khalis, a portly and chatty teen, first introduced the concept. He had been coming to the center for almost a year, when I asked him about the variations he had noticed. His answer reminded me of the mobile hotspots in the living spaces and the contingent influence of their suggestions (chapter two), yet Khalis pinpointed *how* these familiar landmarks varied:

> Well, how to explain it to you? I will call it 'waves'. A new group is shaping, and this group comes to do other things or to use other spaces, and this makes a wave. ... When I arrived, the group already there was often sitting. Or we went to the computer room. And then other teens arrived, and they preferred playing ping-pong, so we migrated over there. So, you see, each group will use the space differently. But, there are always guys remaining from before. ... With the start of the school year, a number of teens left. For some of the newcomers, it was hard to communicate with the rest of the group who had already become acquainted. It must reshape a group. So it varies like that, by waves.

This was interesting. At first glance, a wave simply describes habits and appreciations that vary with the reshaping of the group of teens, while those already there would somehow mingle with newcomers. But to call it a 'wave' created a thought-provoking connection with the phenomenon of ocean waves. Since the early 1960s, Helmreich (2014) notes, oceanographers don't model waves as individual undulations anymore, but "as collections of superimposed waves, little and big, with different origins. A 'wave' might be made up of forces churned up by a hurricane a week ago, as well as by fresh energy from wind-swept ripples" (270). This means that there are different forces that blow on water, with older or newer origins. These forces put water in motion, sparking its movement as a particle detaches from its mass, from the flood, and the warp might meet the swell or vanish on the shore. Khalis probably resorted to 'wave' for its social analogy, as the word also denotes the spread of people, or of a particular interest, opinion, or style (as with the French New Wave cinema). But his depiction, I think, was no stranger to oceanographers' conception of sea waves in that both imply a renewal, with new layers building upon and mingling with previous ones. In the day center, if "there are always guys remaining from before", as Khalid said, if this group is always partially changing, waves never emerge on a *tabula rasa*. Newcomers follow departing teens, and some of them remain, so that familiar affinities within the group keep building upon existing ones, whether with older or newer origins.

When I told caregivers about Khalis' picture of waves, it found meaningful echoes among them. In contrast with the teens, caregivers spent longer periods of time in the center, so they recalled plentiful variations, such as moving activities, rebuilding furniture, repainting walls, replacing artworks, etc. They joked about a special sort of wave they knew all too well: when the yard became decrepit due to a tendency of neglect among the teens, which prompted the organization of a communal restoration of that spot. Their jokes about the yard now clarify the differences between the two photographs that opened this chapter. To the team, waves did not only mean an evolution of familiar habits, but they pervaded workshops as well, and they included all sorts of material rearrangements occurring now and then. Caregivers stressed that such waves made the place "lively", which is the focus of the next chapter. For now, it is worth noting that waves erode: they carry material variations.

Yet this statement doesn't explain through which strategy of enrollment a wave erodes; that is, how an interest spreads, grows and materializes in the place while forming a wave. The story of the *Stylistique* workshop helps to figure out how such an informal variation occurs. At the time we were still in the old town house, every Monday morning, the teenagers were offered the option of going to the *Esthétique* workshop in *L'Annexe*, three rooms in a row arranged for creative activities. Among piles of drawing paper, mosaic materials, and paintbrushes, a mirror was placed on a table in a corner, where participants could sit and put on makeup, apply nail polish, or style their hair. Six months later, that material space had changed, as had the workshop's name, now *Stylistique*. Whereas the corner table was still used for beauty activities, other tables were now dedicated to beads and the creation of clothes. With the move to the new building, this latent effervescence grew in an even more striking variation. There, the workshop was honored by its own room. It was arranged with a large mirror fixed on the wall, and contained several tables and shelves full of materials for beauty and dressing, whether it be for hair, clothing, or accessories. I looked into the meeting archives, but nowhere were these amplifications and installations recorded. I brought the question to Berenice, the caregiver who led the workshop. She recalled its variation from the early days in L'Annexe:

> Before we had this part with the cosmetics and hairdressing, and the other one with beads and jewelry. But then, at a certain moment, with several girls we got greatly involved in a project that had to do with customizing bags, scarves, etc. ... And we staged a fashion show. We arranged the back room as a dressing room and we paraded in the two front rooms. And from there, we started to think about doing something related to the body, the sewing, and creativity. So it had turned into a mixture, Stylistique.
>
> So when the workshop evolved into Stylistique, I asked her, did this change relate to the teens involvement?

The idea of the 'wave' was familiar to us by that time, so it was no surprise that she picked it up in her answer:

> Yes, I think it was tied to the wave of that group of girls who, at that time, fully embraced everything that had to do with customizing [clothes], a bit more in sewing. But it was a mix — because, still before

that, we added some beads, as Joris [a teenager] really liked it. Not only for jewelry, but he made crocodiles, dolphins, animal figures with beads. And then [when Joris left] we had no more teens who were especially interested in bead figures and it remained only jewelry creation. So we discarded the word 'bead', and added instead 'fashion design' [in French, 'stylisme', so Esthétique became Styli-stique].

While Joris' taste for bead figures remained individual, and was discarded as soon as the youth was gone, the appetite of a group of girls for fashion design manifests how much a wave depended on relationships. A wave arises from social bonds and it needs them to gain sufficient strength. In this sense, participants' enrollment with a 'wave' inevitably passes through the impacts of interpersonal encounters, which occurred with the girls but not with Joris. In her novel *The Waves* (2000 [1931]), Virginia Woolf poetically amplifies our awareness of such interpersonal alterations. Through the course of the novel's narrative, six friends take turns telling moments of the life that they have shared. The continuity of voices is interrupted by depictions of waves at successive times of the day, giving an acute sense of the diverse states through which someone becomes relationally, from one moment to another, from one tide of feelings to another, whether waves ripple, splash, break, crush, drum on the shore, sweep over it swiftly, fall, withdraw, or fall again. The many lyrical pictures in the novel make readers feel how a person's state in the moment is not anecdotal, but part of interpersonal alterations with forces at stake. And the flow of successive waves emphasizes every state's evanescence. In other words, these depictions amplify an awareness of the fleeting sensations that alter someone when in relation with another and, in the same move, that deviate each one's concerns. Waves emerge through these alterations in interpersonal encounters. Back at the Stylistique workshop, this process became clear as Berenice continued the story. Enlarging the scope of these interpersonal alterations helped to settle the variation:

> After the fashion show, she pursued, other caregivers asked if we [Berenice and the participants] would continue, so that we could sell our objects to workers of the institution or relatives. So we also

continued on because we were affirmed [by others] when making them, that [our creations] had become worthwhile.

However, although Stylistique had its heyday, Berenice mentioned as well that, "today, not that much is going on":

It is nice for teens who want to go there", she said, "but there is less force and creativity than at that time.
Well, this is inherent to waves, no? I replied. They entail force and creativity at the time the adolescents are in for it.
Yes, but caregivers too, she reacted swiftly. I was very excited to be involved in that workshop for a while, but I couldn't do it like that for ten years. Repetition is a bit deadly. I cannot inject as much creativity and suppleness when I just repeat the same things. ... For instance, at the present time I am greatly involved in the climbing workshop. I love it, because I see that teens get into it, and because I like to go outside and to see teens outside – there they are not the same people anymore! Well, I guess I also work with waves.

And that was her end of the story. So here is the wave's strategy of enrollment. Khalis already emphasized how familiar affinities varied with the partial reshaping of the group, mingling old and new habits. Coming to workshops, when Esthétique turned into Stylistique, it wasn't an abrupt change either. "It was a mix", Berenice said; the variation built upon a previous teen's involvement in bead creations and deviated, giving more room to sewing and jewelry and less to beads. In the course of that workshop, a wave of creativity formed, and grew stronger, while a taste for some specific activity spread within the group through interpersonal alterations, and then vanished as other waves came by. A wave is thus a temporary interest among several participants, including teens, caregivers, their ephemeral penchants, stuff at hand or the things they come to particularize, and sometimes external enthusiasts. A wave drives certain forms of strength and suppleness, and it causes material variations as participants' interests slightly deviate, rendering a space more specific to the group and to a period of time.

As such, waves capture a way of dwelling that follows teens' and caregivers' interests in quite an informal manner. That is, a wave sustains and transforms teens' and caregivers' interests through their ways of life in the place, since the way they live there (where they go, what they do, and with whom) deviates over time when the group reshapes and its members weave new interpersonal affinities.[6] And when a wave erodes, it carries a spatial variation that instils these specific affinities in the place's materiality. Seen this way, dwelling is not settling down, where the installation or occupation of a place is clearly defined. Perhaps 'strategy' is a too strong word for the subtle interplays of enrollment with a wave. The enrollment of participants and things in waves occurred when forces and alterations moved through mundane moments of daily life in the care center. Compared to the caregivers' exchanges and their debates with the adolescents, waves did not occur when reporting about those daily events, nor when teenagers were asked to express ideas in meetings. Here, the recreation of shared interests is directly bonded to the material suggestions of the living spaces that enabled the formation of contingent familiar bonds, and to the workshop framings that offered passages for participant involvement, increasing the teens' possibilities to develop certain penchants while leaving out others. Waves intimately rely on these daily affinities. When a minor attachment spreads into greater interest among the group members, a wave is a variation that increases the existence of that attachment – that gives more room to it figuratively and materially – in the ongoing care practice and its place.

---

6   Ingold (2011 [1995]) argues that 'dwelling' is a central constituent in the processes of building environment. These processes are always specific to a dwelling, whether by human and nonhuman beings. My descriptions sound very similar to his argument, except that in the day center, material transformation through dwelling is a great stake for a situated practice, and for this reason I would not hold it as a universal truth about situations across cultures, epochs, and species.

From the slightest attachment

The exploration of the variations of caregivers' and teenagers' interests leads us to a crucial turning point of this book. Whether occurring through the noticing and reports of intriguing occurrences to colleagues, discussions in community meetings, or informal waves, these strategies of enrollment outline 'interest' as a form of attachment that depends on slighter forms of affinities, such as everyday familiar bonds or involvement in workshops. Such inclinations are slighter because they happen in the moment, whereas an interest cements over time as it spreads within the group. A slight attachment can take the form of an opportunistic and contingent response an adolescent gives to a material suggestion in the living spaces (chapter one), or it can take shape as a passage into a state of greater attention, curiosity or bodily sensation in a workshop, however uncertain and unstable this involvement may be (chapter three). These day-to-day appreciations not only feed caregivers' informal knowledge, enabling them to craft particular therapeutic paths with the teens, but these penchants also have important consequences for care work, and for institutional life and its place. I will now end this chapter by considering these latter consequences.

Enrollment into a shared interest could erupt not only from slight attachments, but even from the slightest one. Next to the permanent workshops, whose variations remained internal, next to the typical tastes of adolescents that barely surprised the team (sports, music, and video games were common), and next to a youth's singular expertise that promised therapeutic potential (Gery's skills in bike repair), the slightest of attachments also manifested in a gesture (a dance step in front of a mirror); an alteration emanating in interpersonal encounters (as the one infusing a taste for fashion design); or in contact with some new thing (like when wrapping in a fabric support). These slight attachments could spark interests that might grow into new activities or spatial arrangements. I gradually came to understand that what truly mattered in the care work was not the realization of an interest in an activity and space *per se*, but rather how the slightest of teenagers' appreciation could nourish the care work. Every little affinity of a youth could count, *at every possible degree*, if caregivers noticed their emergence in day-to-day interactions between the teens and their surroundings.

Indeed, I heard many propositions voiced that were, after all, never accomplished. Many emerging interests did not make the care practice or material spaces vary. At least during the year following the one I spent in the center, the hip-hop workshop was eventually not planned, and the fabric supports were never hung from the relaxation room ceiling. So what was the point of these failures? Were the caregivers too lazy, busy, or unconcerned by these zones of interests they encountered with teens and that environment? I do not think so. I see it rather as a particularity of that institution's enrollment processes: it was always a matter of cultivating an awareness of possibilities, even if all of them were not realized.[7] So the important point was not the realization of every spark of interest into practical or spatial variations. Anyway, the realization of these possibilities was limited; remember the flexible chart whose columns (especially the side one) were finite. Money and time obviously set limits too. Some caregivers told me they could not be incessantly inventive over time, or they would risk exhaustion. The important point for caregivers was to remain open to emerging possibilities, to cultivate their awareness of them, sometimes enrolling teens into this awareness too. Then, perhaps, would they experiment with the realization of a possibility in the care practice. It was caregivers' awareness of the sensitivity of each adolescent, even in its minimal expression, that ingrained their spaces and practice with care.

Although all possibilities didn't set off a strategy of enrollment, enough of them were realized so that the everyday activities and in-

---

7   In her study of dementia wards in the Netherlands, Driessen (2020) calls "sociomaterial awareness" (233) a sensitivity of caregivers to the ways in which the built environment enables residents to engage in better ways of living. The team continuously adjusts the environment according to day-to-day situations they deem problematic. In the day center, the caregivers' understanding of the teens' penchants as possibilities for becoming greater interests therefore appears as one sort of socio-material awareness. Here, this sensitivity is bonded to the stake of working with the appreciations that come to matter between teens and professionals.

stitutional place were attuned to interests current in the group. Slight attachments were thus not only consequent for the way the care work was done. These modest appreciations, when growing into interests among caregivers and teens, enabled them to make the institutional life and place specific to their attachments that consolidated, dissolved, and reconstituted over time. These variations rendered the activities and spaces interpersonally meaningful to the teens and caregivers. None of them were either interchangeable nor replaceable in the care work once they were caught in the particular world of these interpersonal encounters, daily occurrences, stories about them, and possibilities that emerged from them.

This chapter ends by calling attention to the subject of place-making along changing uses.[8] Here, this subject manifests from a sharp angle: when the place is materially and discursively rendered specific to the declining and rekindling of its dwellers' interests over time. The process departed from a building that was typologically hybrid and whose rooms' diverse purposes were partially undefined. Each variation that the team arranged with the teens increased the hybrid, atypical character of the building. Along with each individual, they cultivated the place's specificities in close relation to their present interests.

This collective particularization of the place, then, seemed never to happen in the manner of a *tabula rasa*. A variation through interest is not a 'change'. The latter implies a sense of renewing, of full replacement with something else. Quite the contrary, a variation was always a partial rearrangement of a spot. The caregivers' strategy of enrollment depended on their relay of unpredictable day-to-day occurrences, on smooth exchanges or tense confrontations in meetings with teens, and

8   Too many works in the social sciences could be cited about this subject, so let me restrict the scope to those that sharpened my view on such processes. I have already referred to Ingold (2011 [1995]) and Driessen (2020) above, but see also Gieryn's description (2002) of a university building that provides certain conditions of uses and remains open to its material reconfiguration, or Guggenheim's analysis (2013) of the conversions of sacred buildings. See also d'Hoop (2016) for an analysis of what I termed "design through use" (37) in four different psychiatric facilities.

on waves that built upon previous habits or involvements of the group members, which then mingled with new ones. In this way, a variation differs from an 'appropriation', which accentuates the making of one's own thing from something that initially belongs to someone else.[9] It follows, too, that sustaining interest requires an amount of time that can hardly be known in advance; variations occur over long periods of time, whose determinacy remains unsettled since they are strongly dependent on ever-varying groups, persons, and interests. The varying interests, and their evanescence though time, call upon us to dig further into the temporalities of attachment, and the spatial liveliness they carried.

---

9   As Segaud, Brun and Driant (2002: 27–30) summarize, core to the notion of 'appropriation' is the idea of psychological, moral or affective property of space by individual users. For a recent questioning of this presupposition, see Despret (2021 [2019]). In her investigation of birds' territories and of studies about them, she argues that animal appropriations of space through their bodily markings not only appropriate it, but also render themselves proper to it, blurring the distinction between their 'selves' and a place.

Chapter 5
Liveliness with artworks

While the caregivers and teens made the material spaces vary over time, one particular way of doing these variations turned especially problematic with the transition to the new building: that of "putting stuff on walls". Although there was a consensus that rooms had to remain open to rearrangement, the display of artworks fueled tensions. When I brought up the issue of exhibits in a staff meeting, I did not expect to stumble on a great topic of disagreement. The neat white walls of the new building opened a debate on the right aesthetic style that would build up on them. The medical director (Dr B.) made immediately clear to the team that she had already envisioned this style together with the architects:

> Dr B.: Yes, this had been decided. ... It is clear that we won't stick stuff on walls, or nail stuff in walls, or repaint a wall or a door, not for a while. At least, not until I'll be there.
> We turned our heads, looking at the walls of the old townhouse where we still found ourselves at that time. Several posters were pinned here and there along the walls, and a few handmade collages announced the next radio program led by a group of teenagers for a workshop.
> Ingrid: Like this, those posters, to stick stuff on walls – or graffiti?
> Dr B.: No.
> Ingrid: What!? No decoration?
> Dr B.: It will be necessary to hang one billposting board, somewhere. We've asked for picture rails on all continuing walls, in the aim of hang-

ing up some frames. ... This is for when we want to organize an exhibition. ... And not for having stuff like this [she pointed the collages], stuff of all sorts, of all forms, and here I think that Hugo [the artist-sociotherapist] won't contradict me.

Voices stormed the room in a fierce brouhaha. Hugo kept quiet. The doctor continued:

The proposition would also be, at least for some spots – for example, the corridors – to have some frames of the same dimension. A beautiful frame. And with the possibility of change with each exhibition. But with something that serves as a constraint. ... And the constraint will be the same frame size, and another one will be to assort colors. [...] Everybody is not allowed to do any fancy things they want in the building. Otherwise, in six months, it won't look like anything. This can be discussed, but I think that things must be uniform.

Following this, the brouhaha resumed with greater intensity.

I better understood afterward what prompted the clash and the team's fervent response. The aesthetic style that the medical director wanted to implement, one that was uniform in format, assorted in color, and followed scheduled exhibitions, threatened another style that caregivers held to. To them, these artworks imparted a sort of 'liveliness' that permeated the material space. Caregivers often repeated that "it [the place] has to remain lively". The opposing aesthetic styles promoted different relationships with the place and its inhabitants, and fostered different situations in the everyday practice. The medical doctor argued that uniformity and temporal organization would promote a professional environment and, accordingly, professional ways of relating with each other. That argument was not just her fancy. It can be understood from her external position, necessary for guiding the team. In contrast to the caregivers, who remained in the daily practice with its many affects and concerns, she came only a few hours a week for staff meetings. She was thus far less aware of every development of the temporary waves passing through the group, and of the small everyday occurrences that caregivers related. He role was rather to give a fresh perspective, and to analyze the adolescents' conditions from her biomedical knowledge background. On the other hand, the caregivers argued that the artworks should generate "something lively" within the place, in line with the liveliness occurring with the things, teens, and caregivers who spent their days there. The move brought the risk of not reproducing this liveliness in the new building. And this, for the team, was unacceptable. The clash between the two aesthetic styles interrogated the possibility to relay the place's specificities, in two ways: the medical director's ability to be sensitive to caregivers' everyday concerns for teens' slightest and growing attachments and, in turn, their ability to convey to her, as a more external worker, these issues from their daily practice.

The clash led me to examine different artworks, like drawings, paintings, sculptures, frames, posters, mosaic tiles, and expression boards. Along this chapter, I scrutinize whether their aesthetic style would impart 'liveliness', and whether they would lose it when translated into uniformed, assorted, and organized exhibits. I am equally interested in the caregivers' ability to distinguish that some things were 'livelier' than others, and the differences these special things made in their care practice. How was "putting stuff on walls" creating "something lively"? And how did it relate to care concerns? Although the term first remained a bit vague, I came to understand that the plea for 'liveliness' related to an aesthetic style that was contingent on the formation of attachments among adolescents, whether as familiar bonds, momentous involvements or longer-lasting interests. This liveliness was threatened by a scheduled temporality, as exhibitions organized in structured periods of time would thwart it. While the previous chapter ended by pointing to the importance of making the place specific to its dwellers, the following stories will call attention to the temporalities of attachments, instilled with the materiality of artworks. But before turning to art exhibits, I first want to better circumscribe how liveliness is realized, or not, within different traits of the material environment, and its implications for care.

Did you say 'something lively'?

Caregivers' use of the word 'liveliness' was more often intuitive than explicit,[1] and they did not only attribute it to artworks within their material environment. They also pointed to liveliness when a spot was momentarily animated with many movements and interactions, what I previously called 'hotspots' (chapter two). The erosions of waves were other kinds of informal variations over time, yet leaving material traces, that contributed to liveliness as well (chapter four). The names of the center's different rooms also played their part. In the old house, these names did not strictly indicate the function of a room, nor did they allude to therapy. Instead they were brought in by the teens. They often remained within the oral culture of the day center, like with 'La Porte Bleue' (the Blue Door) or 'L'Annexe'. Though no one remembered exactly who had nicknamed these rooms nor how, these appellations were familiar to everyone in the group. Most of these nicknames disappeared with the transition to new building. Some caregivers contested the plaques that had been affixed next to doors, which indicated the room's function: however imprecise and thereby open to changing activities (chapter four), the names were too impersonal to make the place lively. Only La Porte Bleue survived in the new building, because its appellation came to designate not only the spot but the singular pedagogic project itself. The name, the room and the project could not be disentangled. Its new door was painted blue, too.

Also, a little disorder did a great deal to generate liveliness. Caregivers described the unruly objects that permeated the old house as "traces of life, of passages", that were significant "even if it is a little messy". They contrasted such disorder, however small, with places that

---

1   In French, the team used the word '*vivant*' to say 'it is something lively' ('*c'est quelque chose de vivant*'). This word twins both English meanings of 'alive' and 'lively'. I have chosen to translate '*vivant*' into 'lively' because 'lively' sounds close to what I heard in caregivers' concerns: that is, living in the sense of being animated, filled with activity, interest, and excitement.

looked like a good representation of a nice, clean, and aseptic rehabilitation center. They often talked about their own houses to convey to me
this sense of liveliness, whether they introduced themselves as messy
people or not.[2] Indeed, when the bright new building loomed, the team
challenged the assumption that a clean and aseptic environment would
be an improvement.[3] This critique closely resonates with Barrett's (1996:
22–37) description of such an environment in a psychiatric facility. He
links its details of clean and beautifully assorted arrangements to the
idea of "progress". In contrast, other buildings situated further back
on the same institutional site which were run down, or older wards
dedicated to confinement or to chronic patients, were intended for
people less eligible for prestigious clinical work, and symbolized regression. Goffman (1961) already recognized this spatial organization of
progress and regression as structuring "patients' careers". The temporal
and moral dimension of 'progress' that these authors see in the material details of well-ordered and shiny facilities echoes the caregivers'
call for a lively aesthetic style in the day center. This style would avoid
making their place convey this idea of progress within a very modern

---

2   The caregivers' comparison with their own houses recalls the blurred bounda-
     ries between domestic habitats and institutions (chapter two), now in how mat-
     ters of hygiene and messiness are similar or differ in the very details of their
     arrangements. This is reminiscent of Guedez (2004) who shows how the link
     between messiness and aesthetic style is deposited differently in homes' ar-
     rangements. The location of a veranda is a good example of that. She notes
     that, in farmers' houses, order and cleanness matter a lot for aesthetics, so ve-
     randas at the entrance enable undressing without dirtying the interior spaces.
     In contrast, in second residences of the same rural region, verandas open on a
     view that appeals for contemplation, and disorder is seen positively as a lively
     thing.
3   As Laws (2009) reports from a self-help group in England, this critique also ani-
     mates the alternative project pointing out the pitfalls of institutional facilities.
     They denounce the mismatch between caregivers' and patients' aesthetic sen-
     se: the group rejects the institutional spaces with the "niceties of the therapy
     room", as the "misjudged offer of comfort (the 'hideous flowery furnishings' in
     the hospital dayroom, perhaps) trivializes the injury" (1832). The group rather
     defends an aesthetic that "suits the mood" of patients (ibid).

and professional environment, not to mention the connotations about hospitals it carries. This chapter will provide evidence for this research track: it will become clear that the liveliness embedded in artworks does not correspond to the linear improvement that the notion of 'progress' entails.[4] Instead, a lively aesthetic style opens onto more diverse ways to enact time. In this way, it counteracts the so-called exemplarity of modern facilities.

The hotspots, waves, nicknames, and relative disorder of the old house provided the place with interpersonal tones that were quite novel to strangers, since they were specific to the teens' and caregivers' familiarity and current interests. As such, these characteristics shifted their relationship to the building away from a sense of place that was impersonal and exclusively professional, away from a showcase of a modern facility devoted to progressive clinical work. Back to the caregivers' critique of the exemplar and fake aspect of the new building they'd soon move to Maud distinguished different periods in order to ease her colleagues' worries. "It will be first a space of representation", she said, underlining the new, shiny arrangement of the very new building, "but then it will come back to life".

For years, the display of artworks had been pivotal for cultivating the place's lively style. I first considered those creations in terms of temporality when reading a trace of a conversation about them in a meeting report, dating from a year before my fieldwork. The secretary had noted,

---

4   A number of scholars have doubted the Modern assumption about linear time in past decades. They question its assertion of a march forward, going from an archaic past towards future improvement, that belongs the tale of 'progress'. In this chapter I will refer to Serres and Latour (1995), as well as to Rose's (2004) decolonial reading of the implementation of progress, with its linear time and its dynamic of replacement and exclusion. See also Tsing (2015) who calls us to investigate, inside "capitalist ruins", the diverse rhythms of lifeways that have been ignored because they do not fit into the pulse of progress, like those relying on salvage. For a historical study about non-linear representations of time, defying our imagination to span beyond the all too conventional 'timeline', see Rosenberg & Grafton (2010).

"An exhibition is limited in time, so that it doesn't become trivial. [...] Exhibitions need to keep turning, removing works and hanging up others." This note indicated that variations of artworks over time were important to prevent the space from falling into mundanity. So the liveliness enacted with artworks could also be a matter of temporality. In other words, the liveliness of that materiality related to a form of thrill that very likely faded over time; some things were related to current concerns, whereas others no longer did. Such distinction recalls the conceptual difference between 'things' and 'objects' (Latour 2004): a 'thing' is created by participants who bring it into existence, and maintain it by incorporating matters of concerns, meanings, stories, and requests for care. An 'object', in contrast, is matter without values embedded in it. Van Hout, Pols and Willems (2015: 1208) propose to transport this distinction in order to look at everyday objects and things according to the concerns at stake in practices of care. Likewise, these artworks required a description of their materiality as 'things', because their liveliness hinged on their relations to caregivers' and teens' concerns, as long as these concerns remained at stake. Losing those concerns, they might easily become 'objects' deprived of value. The length of time needed was not stipulated in the meeting report, nor in any meeting I attended. This temporal indeterminacy, one might easily suppose, put the organization of exhibitions envisioned by the medical director on a knife's edge. Let us look to how this occurred: how artworks gained or lost their lively character, both during the transition period and while progressively decorating the white walls of the new building for about a year. Let us examine how these things generated liveliness as different temporalities unfolded through them, due to the making of attachments in the care work.

Folding moments of workshops

It was late afternoon and we had not yet moved into the new building. While leaving, I passed by L'Annexe, near the old townhouse, peered through the open door into the creation room, and saw Hugo who was still packing up stuff in the middle of a mess. He was preparing artworks to hang on the naked white walls of the new building. He had already refused my offer to help him, because he said he knew what was what, and what must remain or not, or go with what, and I did not. The stuff in the room was objects to me and things to him. But it was late, and he needed assistance with technical tasks, as he was not used to assembling frames. So he accepted my help and we ended up preparing the artworks, mostly drawings and paintings, that fit in the new frames. This was how I learned more about the concerns and stories that made these artworks worthy of being displayed, and in what sense these values would infuse their liveliness.

The first topic we discussed was the pace at which an exhibition varies. Hugo was an artist hired as a sociotherapist, so he was the main caregiver in charge of the Creation workshop. With that workshop, he told me, he tried to do a new exhibition on average every four months. But in reality, he said, 'trying' meant that he succeeded in holding at least one exhibition a year. So the pace varied from, say, every four months to once a year. That varying pace depended on how the workshop went, and this remained completely unpredictable to him. Four months was too short to produce good enough paintings, but a year was long enough to put teens' sustained interest at risk. This is why the display of artworks could hardly fit in the stiff planning of a calendar: their creation relied on the adolescents' involvement, and thus on the unknown period of time during which their interest for a same activity would be sustained, especially given the strategies of enrollment that could produce variations (chapter four). In other words, the pace of an exhibition was unpredictable because it depended on a collection of short moments when the teens engaged in creating artworks. That collection became possible when enough pieces were achieved, yet before boredom settled.

The importance of the teenagers' involvement appeared with even more nuance when Hugo started selecting certain paintings and drawings out of a heap of different works, and made me aware of other values that were embedded in these artworks. When the time of an exhibition came, he told me, he discussed the choice of artworks to be exhibited with the group of teenagers who produced them. Together they looked for compromises between different concerns. First, Hugo valued the teens' presence: each one who attended the workshop deserved to see their work displayed. Second, he weighed the degree of involvement of each participant when crafting the artwork. As he showed me the paintings, he recounted anecdotes from these moments. Like this flower that fascinated Karina when she painted it. Or all these small dots that had asked so much patience of Eduardo. Or this stain that Joachim finally found a way to integrate into the composition of his image. And, do you recognize which famous picture inspired Kais' drawing? And so forth. One anecdote after another, I came to see how each artwork related to finer nuances and moments, encompassing when a youth chose materials, used tools, took a chance to express ideas or feelings, discussed these with other participants, and was involved in the gestures of making the object. Those very involvements in the practice of crafting things during the workshop particularized the objects that Hugo selected as artworks. After that, he evaluated the visual appearance of the pictures, considering what was good looking and well crafted. The final decision involved trying to find a balance between different techniques, styles, and tints, and between sober and busy pictures.

When Hugo and his participants evaluated which artworks were worth becoming exhibits, the nuances of their involvement when crafting them first mattered, whereas the 'beauty' of their visual appearance and the diversity in their assortment came after. In his study of a Parisian reinsertion facility, Troisoeufs (2009: 107) notices those values in a similar order except that, in his case, bad-looking artworks were displayed as well, but more discreetly. Ugly stuff could earn its place for the moral motive of not excluding the workshop participants who had tried. This detail adds a layer to tinkering with the constraint of a good visual appearance. It insists on the recognition of patients' personal involvement, which is definitely deemed more worthy by caregivers, compared to the artistic mastery of their creation. As to Hugo's selection, his compromise was pressured by frictions about aesthetic style due to the move, where uniformity should reign. Even so, he kept the value of personal involvement in the crafting process at the fore, not in opposition to visual beauty and diversity, but in interdependence with these other values.[5]

What does the story of Hugo preparing the artworks say about the 'liveliness' they entail? The artworks first relate to the experience of creating and the involvement that teens put into making them. In this way, they render the pace of new exhibitions unpredictable, and they require a compromise with other values, like visual beauty. Most of all, Hugo's selection shows that these things remain lively as long as they carry anecdotes about those workshop moments with them, often visible in their appearance (like the dots, or the inspirational picture). The participants who were present at that time would see the anecdotes in the pictures more than their aesthetic aspects. While these pictures are particularized because they incorporate moments in the workshops, these things 'fold' time. That is, they carry past stories with them, gathering places and temporalities that remain visible in their materiality. Anthropologist of science Amade M'Charek (2014) argues, in her historical analysis of a DNA reference sequence, that certain objects deserve consideration for the way they index and enact time. From these 'folded objects' (ibid), she writes, quoting Serres and Latour (1995), traces of previous moments and places cannot be erased:

> In contrast to linear time, which is related to geometry, topological time is crumpled and folded in multiple ways. Time is gathered together and folded in objects (Serres & Latour 1995). 'An object, a circumstance, is thus polychronic, multi-temporal, and reveals a time that is gathered together, with multiple pleats' (1995: 60). [...] Time materializes in spatially foldable objects. Folded objects are not political because of what is put into them, but because of how they are folded. (M'Charek 2014: 31; 50, original emphasis)

---

5   The idea that good care requires seeking compromise between several values belongs to many other kinds of care work. For this argument about food in nursing homes, see Mol (2010), and about 'dignity' in relation to dirtiness in a long-term psychiatric setting, or to end of life care, see Pols (unpublished manuscript).

Reading these lines, it becomes clear that the folding of particular moments of workshops in the artworks did matter, as long as these moments enlivened these things with concerns for the teenagers who made
them, and for the caregivers who shared the workshops with them. Those
who weren't aware of these special moments would notice the content of
the picture, its subject, form and style, but not the stories of its creation.
Hugo' selections leave no doubt: the liveliness of these artworks first relies on these particular craft experiences, whose moments are enfolded
in the artworks displayed.

Things that bring up stories

During the months following the move, artworks were indeed displayed
in frames next to the uniform assortment of furniture. To caregivers and
teens, the twenty or so frames hanging on picture rails did not strongly
enough counterbalance the evocation of a hospital that was produced by
the white walls (figure 19). Yet, the team did not want to solve it in one go.
It was a matter of time, but not of a formally organized time; artworks
should slowly permeate back into the space here and there, at the irregular pace of turning exhibitions. When I came back six months later,
small variations had occurred at several locations. Some of the framed
pictures had been replaced. Posters relating to activities had been hung.
Some stone tiles of a terrace had been replaced by mosaic squares (figure 20). And so on. At that time, teens who had not known the former
old townhouse told me in interviews that the new place did not make
them think of a hospital. The artworks were major contributors to these
impressions, they added, and it helped some of them keep coming back
during the early weeks of their stay.

Figure 19: The frames on the walls of the corridor, after moving into the new building.
Figure 20: The mosaics permeated a side terrace, six months after moving in.

When I asked Baptiste, the coordinator, about these things that slowly permeated the place, he answered that it would have been inappropriate to uproot and 'transplant' all artworks from the former old townhouse to the new building. All of them did not make sense anymore in the flow of interests that were occurring during that time. Indeed, the pieces that Hugo first transported from the old townhouse were freshly crafted, carrying recent moments of workshops. The artworks that made the move, and also the ones that began to permeate the new place over time, all related to current interests and relationships between teenagers and caregivers.

Other artworks, though, were much more vulnerable candidates for moving, and some of them never reached the new building. The transition was a radical checkpoint for turning certain things into mere objects. These futile artworks indicated another feature of lively style, this time, because they'd lost it. This stood out during the selection (or rather, rejection) process, just before the move. In a corner of the old townhouse, two caregivers had gathered artworks from here and there, so that everyone who passed by could check if one of them was worth being saved from the trash. The ensemble of sculptures, paintings, stained glass and collages was colorful. The objects were well fashioned. Some even presented vivid details that caught observers' attention. But the problem was, they lacked the stories. When team members or teens contemplated them, unanswered questions lingered: who was involved in crafting them, when, and how? No one could tell from looking at these obsolete objects. No one remembered exactly which stories were connected to them. In contrast to Hugo's anecdotes, here the pieces did not divulge the faintest reminiscence. These objects faced oblivion since their creators had left the center and, after a while, narratives about them had stopped circulating within the group. In short, these objects were no longer lively because they didn't bring up any more stories to tell.

Then how would 'successful' pieces of artwork do so? And what of the stories that enlivened them? Why did they matter? A photo album made of plastic pouches that hung on the wall worked very well for recalling anecdotes, perhaps because it made directly visible the moments having marked the participants, who thereafter narrated them. The photographs not only showed teens and caregivers posing in diverse attitudes, but they also involved sites, things, and animals that they appreciated, and whose traces they retained and exhibited. It was striking, when some teens told me the stories I could glimpse on the pictures, how much their narrative kept track of the ever-changing members of the group. They always delivered with precision, not only moments they had shared with others, but whether those persons still came to the center or not. The storytellers often repeated that this or that person was not present anymore, but that other one was, or they would ask: were you already there at that time? Were you there where we went on that outing? Did you know Dorian? The stories recorded the reshaping of the group and the temporary interpersonal affinities that resulted from it.

More importantly, some displayed things carried liveliness because the stories they sparked brought back past occurrences or interests, for some of them were still manifest among the group members. Baptiste was serious about this, as the tension in his voice signaled when he told me about a poster of a video game stuck on the wall of the room for media workshops:

> It makes sense when teenagers and caregivers dwell in this place and so bring materials. [...] Etienne and Sylvie [both caregivers] have taken this initiative [to pin the poster] because they involve themselves, because they do this workshop here, and the poster is linked to that workshop. So it's not for the appearance, but it makes sense. In contrast, Dr B. is less often here. Maybe her concern for 'beauty' takes the upper hand over this meaning that the thing carries. When she comes in the room and sees the poster, she probably won't think that it occurred during that workshop, that Etienne proposed it, that Gregory [teenager] brought it, and so it matters for Gregory, and for Etienne, and for the workshop. She'll probably only see that this poster is ugly. If I'll recount it to her, she will understand. But she only comes here for the [weekly] staff meetings. Then she sees the building, without living in it.

The story of the poster is a tiny one, but it is the story of an irreplaceable specificity for these caregivers, this teenager, and that workshop. The poster wasn't part of an exhibition that workshop participants prepared for months. Instead, it had a special mode of presence for Etienne, Sylvie and Gregory since it carried an interest that had emerged between them and a video game. The thing was of concern for Baptiste, too. As a member of the group, he'd been told about the anecdote and knew the story folded in it. In other words, when telling a story, caregivers and teens unfolded the moments the thing contained. They transmitted the importance of these moments to interlocutors who then became aware of these concerns. This meant that caregivers' daily exchanges didn't only bear consequence for their informal knowledge of the teens (chapters two and three), and for possible variations of interest between them (chapter four), but these exchanges resulted, too, in producing concern for the things that surrounded their working place in a lively manner.

However, that mode of presence was not perceivable by someone who did not 'live' there, who did not know all the anecdotes of what happened in the daily practice, such as the medical director. Here the story can do something that the thing cannot: it can reach an external interlocutor and convey to them how meaningful this apparently ugly poster is. This is a precious attribute when the external interlocutor is in a position of topmost authority, like psychiatrists. The poster is pinned to the wall, but the story can travel and can possibly convince the unfamiliar people to whom it is addressed. So things that led to anecdotes did not only re-iterate the importance of an interest that settled in the group. The stories also enabled that importance to be conveyed to those who didn't share the everyday care concerns embedded in these things, and who risked considering them as objects or reducing them to their visual appearance.

With the unwanted artworks, the photo album, and the poster, I saw a second way that displayed things generated liveliness or did not. They did so when they triggered a sort of ordinary storytelling, which appeared as a practice of expanding the present time. In other words, the displayed things that were good at making people tell stories reconnected other moments to the present one and expanded it. These stories kept alive concerns that were important for present and former 'dwellers', while reconnecting them through narrative webs. Thus, these things do not belong to a single linear temporality. They are caught in the different connections relating previous moments, prompting people to tell narratives, to unfold moments. This was how these things maintained their worth and existence in the center, as they kept track of ever-varying interests. In doing so, they carried liveliness, since they marked which concerns remained important in the flow of the ever-changing group of 'dwellers'.

Traces of fleeting gestures

Other exhibits also proved vulnerable to the new aesthetic requirements of uniformity and time organization, but not because concerns about them had vanished and they lacked stories – quite the reverse. In the old townhouse, a chalkboard covered part of the wall of the entrance hall. Teens could write whatever they wanted on that board. The thing varied intensively in the inscriptions that the adolescents and sometimes caregivers traced on it. Since that thing mediated frequent interactions and offered lots of variations of its visual appearance, it should surprise nobody that the team saw it as extremely lively. Yet its reproduction in the new building was not obvious to all. The brief, casual, fleeting involvements that the chalkboard appealed to were, and remain, under debate.

Here is how it happened. Two years before the move, the caregivers and adolescents had decided to cover an area of wall with blackboard paint, in order to make a free expression board for the teens, some of whom painted it. Each time I came back to the field, I noticed new chalk inscriptions, which offered clues to the usages of that board. Once, it was full of small drawings and writing, all slanting in different directions. When looking at them, I discerned that they were from different hands. The subjects of the pictures and notes responded to each other by association of ideas or by making jokes. Another time, a line in the middle of the board divided its surface into two parts. On each side, a big character had been drawn, partly human, partly not. On the left, the mysterious character had a human body with peculiar long arms, and something hardly identifiable across his mouth. The character on the right was about the same size. It was a genie out of the lamp, with quite well-trained pectoral and arm muscles, and with boxing gloves on. It was signed on the side with a nickname. At other times, seeing new sketches on the board, again I recorded that earlier inscriptions suggested the making of later ones. The visual appearance of the board indicated that teens had been caught up in brief involvements, writing on the board when passing by, in the same move responding to previous inscriptions. The blackboard was a mediator of sociability (inscriptions were responding each other) and of interactional creativity (most of the ideas, visible in the drawings and notes, were inspired by each other), while this thing engaged us in very brief, casual involvements. Writing with chalk demanded simple, ephemeral gestures, quick ideas, often inspired by what was there in the moment, and inscriptions were quickly erasable as well.

The chalkboard's materiality was indispensable to these spontaneous and quick gestures. It was not quite the same thing, to say the least, as another expression board made of cork. Caregivers had hung the corkboard in the former dining room, with a note pinned next to it: "Billposting permitted. This is a space of free expression, for individual posting, and for at least two weeks." Half of the available area was empty. And I barely noticed a change in the three drawings that covered the other half of the board. The cork panel appeared as an object that had been largely forgotten by all. In comparison, the materiality of the painted chalkboard made a great difference to its popularity. To write a note or draw with chalk on the wall appealed to spontaneous and brief gestures, possibly responding to previous inscriptions, whereas the cork panel, the pushpins, and the note stating the conditions for individual postings surely had no chance to do so. The cork panel could not lure casual and fleeting gestures of writing and ephemeral inscriptions as responses to previous ones. As such, it didn't generate liveliness as the chalkboard did.

But that way of enacting liveliness was very fragile. During a meeting before the move, the chalkboard raised a fierce debate. The doctors had decided to remove it from the architects' plans. They argued that the board had been used randomly, without being framed as a 'therapeutic mediation'. This rendered it wholly inadequate for the new building. They named the thing a "call for discharge". According to a dictionary of psychology, this expression points to a liberation, an emotional explosion, that occurs when a phase of psychological tension ends (Richelle 2007 [1991]). By resorting to that expert term, the doctors asserted their position of authority.[6] To them, the thing dirtied the beautiful new place while triggering irrelevant attitudes among the adolescents. Part of the team tried to plead for its relevance. One of them raised the argument that "the teens also put interesting things on it", without digging into what was interesting in those things. The caregiver had only furtive moments at hand, not enough to form a good anecdote. Another one pointed out that, even if writing on walls was not allowed, teenagers would do it anyway, so why not to set up a spot for it? These arguments were made in vain. Though the team didn't convince the psychiatrists, they didn't want to prevent the chalkboard from demonstrating its worth. They finally decided to leave the question open for later: if the teenagers asked for an expression board again, the question would be reconsidered.

I kept coming back to the center for a year and a half after the move and never saw the chalkboard reproduced in the new building. The board only came back as a concern when the team discovered a small doodle on a corner of wall or on the door of a toilet, which caused them to resume the debate. Or occasionally, during Christmas time, ideas of what the board encouraged teens to do (casual involvement in writing or drawing inscriptions that remained easily erasable) came back with liquid chalk pens that they used on window panels. However, to my knowledge, the team never recreated a wall covered with chalkboard paint.

---

6   Studies that expose how psychiatrists establish their superior position vis-à-vis care teams are too numerous to be encapsulated in a note. Close to my observation, Brodwin (2013) points that psychiatrists' verbal performance, often resorting to biomedical knowledge, prompts case managers to accept that they know less, although their own knowledge is just of different kind. More broadly, Carr (2010) offers a review of anthropological works that unravels how expertise is something that is performed, in the medical field and elsewhere.

The chalkboard was fragile because it did not offer a guarantee of an aesthetic style that would showcase a professional facility. At any moment, a teen could trace an unsettling joke or a crappy word, and this would, according to the medical directors, dirty the modern building. Above all, the chalkboard was fragile because the brief gestures to which it appealed were vulnerable in the face of therapeutic arguments. These casual involvements in writing inscriptions (often unpredictable because of responding to others) were not easy to translate into coherent arguments that would match therapeutic formulations. In contrast with planned workshops, the fleeting gestures and traces on the board were occurrences that did not happen in situations set up on purpose, with minimal framing (chapter three). So far, these occurrences have always existed outside any discursive or argumentative register. The debate about that board brings back a problematic issue of care work: when daily occurrences that happen in the margins of planned activities are deemed unworthy of considering because they are not translated into a discourse, therapeutic or other.[7]

But however arduous the translation of brief and casual involvements into convincing words during debate, it was precisely the board's appeal to these gestures that effected its liveliness. Its materiality mattered: writing with chalk seized people passing by much more spontaneously than pinning a piece of paper onto cork. The chalkboard had a very lively effect in yet another way than by unfolding moments of workshops or prompting storytelling. The board's style relied exclusively

---

7   This is a topical issue among care practices and theorists. Nowhere have I found a more profound insight about it than in the experimentation of Fernand Deligny with autistic children in the 1970s. With his companions, they mapped the children's movements and doings within the surroundings, which made visible the 'act' ('agir', gestures or movements that have no purpose at all) as much as the 'doing' ('faire', gestures or movements with purpose, or whose intentionality is presumed). Such mapping was a way to render visible and important children's attachments in the margins, without interpreting such a non-verbal language with theoretical preconception. See Deligny, Lin & Duran (2013) for the collection of maps, and Miguel (2014) for a concise analysis of that experiment.

on gestures and inscriptions that were ephemeral: writing with chalk is about the moment and quickly erasable. Its ephemerality made it much more vulnerable than other exhibits. But it was exactly because of that ephemerality – because of the brief, evanescent involvements, and the unpredictable traces they left – that the caregivers valued the board as something lively. The subject remained a source of tension, and left the debate among caregivers unresolved.[8]

Overlapping temporalities

As months and then years passed, artworks slowly permeated the walls, and sometimes the floors or doors, of the new building. Together with hotspots, waves, nicknames and a little disorder, the artworks instilled the place with a lively aesthetic style. Their presence, visual appearance, material characteristics, and the stories and doings they prompted, intimately related to the adolescents' attachments, modest as they were. But I need to emphasize this: to say that the artworks 'slowly' permeated the walls is too simple a phrasing to describe how time was involved in that recreation of liveliness.

Indeed, exhibitions never turned according to a schedule, but each of them followed the pace of a workshop. What was 'slow' or 'fast' could no longer be counted on the basis of a stable reference such as a calendar. This pace could hardly be organized in advance, since it remained unpredictable: it depended on the teens' involvement in a particular workshop, and on the sustainment of their interest over time. Forcing these paces into calendars would have thwarted the care work because, as I described in the earlier chapters of this book, this work could hardly do without weaving those teens' attachments. The variations of exhibitions,

---

8   At the other extremity, teens' inscriptions on the building elements that were to stay for an undetermined, long-lasting period, also raised debate among caregivers. They wondered how long traces of an adolescent should remain in the center if the latter had been gone for a while. For the case of a controversy about a painted door, see d'Hoop (2021a).

or of single exhibits, only left a vague impression of linear time passing in the building. According to Latour (1991), when a systematic cohesion of elements of our everyday life replaces others, and forms a new
cohesion, things give the impression that time is linear. I see a good example of these systematic cohesions in the ways smartphones quickly
made mobile phones and landlines obsolete. As for the changing exhibitions in the day center, although they marked that some periods occurred
one after another, each display of an exhibition or of a single piece followed such singular paces that it simply blurred any systematic cohesion
among them. These exhibitions just never held the promise of a uniform
style in the building. Rather, their respective temporalities overlapped.

In this way, the artworks carrying liveliness enacted time in another
manner. Latour (ibid) also argues that, despite the impression of passing
time, the brewing of many temporalities instills material things and the
actions done with them. The exhibits of the day center incorporated this
idea in a specific manner: these things were deemed lively when they unfolded workshop moments, and when they inspired the telling of stories
that expanded the present time to other moments and places. These temporalities belonging to the thing and to its narratives added still another
sort of temporal overlap to the variations of exhibitions. Not only did
these overlaps blur the impression of passing time through systematic
cohesion, but they fully dispelled it, and rather provided a liveliness relying on the much more enfolded and unfolding times that those things
carried. Thus, it seemed to me that the 'something lively' that caregivers
sought to recreate in the new building thanks to artworks wasn't only enacted through the unpredictable paces of renewed exhibitions, but also
through their overlaps with the many different temporalities that these
things carried.

Finally, let us pinpoint how these overlapping temporalities, and
the lively aesthetic style they lend the building, relate to care concerns.
The temporal overlaps obfuscated a linear time that would imply an
idea of progress. It cracked the linear notion of improvement, which
would have manifested in the neat, uniform, modern and apparently
immutable style of a facility arranged as an exclusively professional
environment. The artworks and their multiple temporalities instead

cultivated a lively style by establishing intimate connections between the material environment and the interpersonal affinities temporarily at stake with its dwellers. One of the difficulties, though, was to convey to external interlocutors how important those attachments were to the care work. This difficulty caused serious concerns when medical directors too easily reduced their view of an exhibit to its visual appearance. The telling of anecdotes was a good trick to unfold the concerns recorded in a thing and to create awareness among outsiders. Yet this did not always work. The chalkboard and its traces were perceived as quite lively by the team, but their temporality showed a limit: the fleeting gestures were too brief, too ephemeral, for them to be argued as worthy occurrences in regard to therapeutic discourses. Yet, even if no practical or argumentative framework had been granted to the erasable inscriptions on the chalkboard, for the caregivers who shared that place with teens on an everyday basis, the enactment of such ephemeral affinities did matter. The smallest of those brief appreciations was precisely what enlivened the team' workplace and the teens' existence there.

Epilogue
On subtlety

Listening to the stories of others, anthropologist Deborah B. Rose writes, "is to be drawn into a world of ethical encounter: to hear is to witness; to witness is to become entangled" (Rose 2004: 213). This is what she designates an "ethics of connection" (ibid: 32). Far from formulating general prescriptions, this ethics "requires a 'we' who share a time and space of attentiveness, and who bring our moral capabilities into the encounter" (ibid: 30; see also 213–214). I'll end this book by pointing to some of those ethical implications of the issues and challenges brought up in the stories told in the preceding pages. More precisely, those ethical implications touch upon the *subtlety* that the stories contain.

These pages have provided a sense of how institutional spaces, thanks to their specific arrangements and to caregivers' practice, enable teenagers' affinities to emerge from their slightest degree of existence and, in turn, how those spaces can incorporate these attachments in their materiality. Both the care interactions and material arrangements that allow these slight attachments to emerge have ethical implications because they are subtle. These things and ways of doing are subtle since they imply delicate yet complex values, easily overlooked by those who haven't developed the skills needed to notice and play with them. Therefore, their subtlety raises ethical implications for a "we" that goes beyond my encounter with the members of that particular therapeutic community. Their subtlety holds accountable, too, researchers and practitioners involved in the future of psychiatric care and the spatial organization of residential care institutions, perhaps even more if they are unfamiliar with the daily stakes of these places. In attending to the subtleties of these spaces and attachments – or the lack thereof – it becomes possible for us to pinpoint some of the ethical challenges they raise for psychiatric and institutional care.

When I first met the team and teenagers of the day center, something happened that left me perplexed. I came to a community meeting to introduce my research to them, joining their jagged circle in the dining room of the old house. It was striking how much the participants paid close attention to what was going on during the discussion. The next point in the agenda was the rearrangement of the yard. I wasn't supposed to start ethnographic observations yet, but I couldn't help quickly jotting it down in my journal. A youth glimpsed this gesture, and then looked towards the yard on which the patio doors opened. He let out, visibly tickled by the idea: "Hey, why don't we take advantage of our new trainee in architecture to arrange the yard together with her?!" Without clearly understanding what sounded so uncommon in that response to my gesture, again, I couldn't resist noting it. A few months later, we found ourselves building new benches for the yard. But this is not the consequence that I would like to emphasize with this anecdote. Today I better understand what that teen did and what was puzzling to me. He handled a contingency. That is, he seized a contingency, an occurrence that was both unexpected and unusual, and he responded to it by testing if it would spur others' interest, therefore opening up more possibilities for certain appreciations to be realized. To some extent, the teen had learned to engage in this subtle technique that seems intuitive and implicit in the hands and words of caregivers. The latter handle contingencies when they take advantage of the material space, the social environment, and the unexpected occurrences that happen in a moment when a person is responding to that milieu, with their affinities or dislikes, and then they adjust to those responses. This ability to work with instant contingencies does not mean that caregivers are fully permissive or celebrate teenagers' freedom. Rather, their subtle technique and material surroundings leave room for trying things out with different persons, without guarantees and in unpredictable ways. Two aspects of that care technique help to grasp its subtlety.

First, trying to induce the teenagers' affinities demanded a special attentiveness to everyday occurrences. Caregivers needed availability and time to allow their noticing of the instant emergence of appreciations in day-to-day interactions with the surrounding spaces. They noticed everyday familiar bonds or involvement in workshops when spending time with teens, whereas these affinities appeared trivial to outsiders. Their awareness of teens' sensitivity, even in its minimal expression, permeated their care practice with subtlety. Caregivers' empirical attention was radical, leaving open the question as to from which threshold an attachment might be recognized as sufficiently holding someone to some things.

This special attentiveness to everyday occurrences could be misunderstood as a form of diluted surveillance, as if the panopticon once inscribed in the building had now shifted to an attentive copresence. The team was conscious of this point. They knew well that too much attention, that constantly "being after the teens," as they said, could devastate the equilibrium of their casual relationship, oscillating between invitation and letting go. For instance, when teens' disinvolvement on a sport field led them to recall the framework of the activity, this risked shifting their relationship to a formal and disciplinary one. The team remained aware of that risk, and frequently debated it. The caregivers' ability to perceive teens' affinities and dislikes necessitated keeping that risk in sight, because an excess of attention would undermine the subtle invitations to position themselves and to elicit their affinity.

Second, the handling of contingencies is subtle because it engages the creation of attachments through a play of responses, not only of material spaces or objects when encountering them, but also when teens and caregivers adjusted accordingly. When a teen 'responded' to, say, a displayed painting, or went to a corner to withdraw, other things and group members were reengaged differently. Through this play of responses, streams of personal and collective appreciations varied over time in an unpredictable manner. Imagine, if you will, who could have known that Kevin might be able to "slow down in his bubble" when caring for animals? No one, but Maud eventually proposed for him a traineeship in bird rehabilitation. Or why would a group of girls, at some point, take over a previous teenager's interest in bead creations, and then start customizing clothes? Who knows, but it spawned a wave of *Stylistique* and the erosion of a material variation. And what could predispose Gregory, Etienne, and Sylvie to come across a video game all of them could enjoy? There was no clear idea, but the poster that enfolded the story must stay on the wall. And so on. Whereas the creation of attachments always happens on an unpredictable path (Hennion 2005), here it was especially so because it moved through plays of responses that were both relational – including to a material environment – and personal. In the course of this 'responsive care', caregivers' attentiveness to small and contingent occurrences gives room to what moves teenagers, to what matters to them. This leads caregivers to respond to these unpredictable affinities by envisioning a therapeutic path, adjusting their attitude, or relaying information to the group. Even the most tenuous inclinations can become of greater interest, and bear larger consequences for the care work, institutional life, and its place. Moreover, as I suggested in the first chapter, this play of responses informs and enacts what each youth may become as a relational person, given the possibility to take a position and to experience the consequences of this positioning for others.

These intuitive techniques of crafting attachments from everyday contingencies call for recognition and articulation. Where they still exist in the current psychiatric field, they are vulnerable because the effects of this mode of therapeutic intervention are hard to prove in clear and direct terms. The therapeutic effects of shifting attachments are not suited to be quantified in terms of 'evidence', which is the language of medical discourse. While psychiatric teams often mingle psychodynamic with biomedical practices, this problem of scientific legitimacy renders caregivers' informal knowledge highly vulnerable when confronted with the scientific discourses of biomedicine. At one extreme, by underestimating its subtleties, community work risks not being considered as care at all, instead dismissed as a mere occupational activity. Plus, as public reforms favor the establishment of ambulatory care and mobile teams, this shifting context seems blind to the spatial mediations that, as we have seen, remain crucial in community psychiatry. Ultimately, I see the predominance of biomedicine as a risk to the handling of contingencies and informal learning: it leaves little room for the flourishing of personal affinities, nor for a much more livable and enriched therapeutic care work.

The subtlety of responsive care doesn't only exist in caregivers' attentiveness and intuitive techniques but pervades the material spaces. It is thanks to subtle details of the building and its spaces – a corner, a semi-open kitchen articulated to living spaces, a displayed object – that caregivers can work with the attachments of teenagers. However, the building is not alone in fostering the emergence of appreciations. As time passes, variations of interests and of artworks modify the spatial arrangements. This is how the psychiatry building is made livable and lively: it invites its inhabitants to develop modest attachments, and some of them come to materialize in the space. The transition to the new care building made these subtleties palpable. This vibrant moment of indeterminacy required the caregivers to relay their sense of the place, and this taught us many lessons about their matters of space. But every spatial arrangement was not equally easy to transport from the old townhouse to the new building. It required effort to relay the subtle dimensions of the environment to external people, for those doing the conveying and for those listening. I can now appreciate the importance of many moments when caregivers hesitated about details, whether in the numerous meetings with architects or the contractor, staff meetings, community meetings, visits to the building sites, when sharing their apprehension of the move, or during the installation phase, in the caregivers' shared office or in other nooks. These moments allowed them to pay attention to the old townhouse as an existing material place crowded with values. They allowed them to carefully transport the subtleties of its space and the different forms of attachments it carried to the new building.

By looking at those spatial details retrospectively, we can better perceive the vivid contrast they afford with settings where residents' attachments hardly come into being. Throughout my research, I encountered such places, from acute care units to long-term housing, and caregivers and patients described others to me. Like the desk at the entrance and the long white corridor of the new building that opened this book, their spaces are often woven differently to daily care: they disable the creation of personal affinities, and they enable other sorts of situations, values, and relationships. Bluntly portrayed, these places are sites where everything that is arranged is purely functional, and few objects exceed this functionality. Few spaces are left for unpredictable occurrences like adjusting one's distance. Few displayed things prompt people to tell stories or open the imagination. These places sometimes look like hotels, where settings for comfort are similarly reproduced floor after floor. I heard this referred to as the "serial bedrooms" pattern. Walls may be bare, or decorated with indifference, with paintings that are supposed to meet everyone's taste but actually meet nobody's, giving an impression of waiting rooms. In these places, patients rarely go to the dining room (or rather, the cafeteria) before the precise time to start a line to receive food in plastic boxes. The omnipresence of technological devices displays and enacts the prevalence of security norms over other concerns. The odor of antiseptic products covers other possible smells. And these spaces appear sterile; few variations are noticeable over time. At least in these details, still existing today, many care institutions lack the subtle play of attentiveness and response that animates a place with attachments, that are always personal and collective, and so always specific and temporary. The perspective I offer in this book does not tell us all that we want to know about matters of space in psychiatry, or more generally in care institutions. But I hope it helps us recognize the subtle ways in which these material environments can hold space for their people as persons, and this, from the slightest of their attachments.

References

Ankele, Monika & Majerus, Benoît (eds.) (2020): *Material Cultures of Psychiatry*, Bielefeld: transcript.

Baillon, Guy (1982): "De nos monumensonges à une réalité à construire." In: de Schouwer, Piet & Sand, E. Alfred (eds.), *Architecture et santé mentale. Bruxelles, 17–19 novembre 1981*, Bruxelles: Editions de l'Université Libre de Bruxelles, pp. 112–145.

Barham, Peter & Hayward, Robert (1991): *From the Mental Patient to the Person*, London: Routledge.

Barrett, Robert J. (1996): "Time and Space in a Progressive Psychiatric Hospital." In: *The Psychiatric Team and the Social Definition of Schizophrenia: An Anthropological Study of Person and Illness*, Cambridge: Cambridge University Press, pp. 22–37.

Bellahsen, Mathieu & Knaebel, Rachel (2020): *La révolte de la psychiatrie. Les ripostes à la catastrophe gestionnaire*, Paris: La Découverte.

Bessy, Christian & Chateauraynaud, Francis (1995): *Experts et faussaires. Pour une sociologie de la perception*, Paris: Métailié.

Blundell Jones, Peter, Petrescu, Doina & Till, Jeremy (eds.) (2005): *Architecture and Participation*, London: Spon Press.

Bouchy, Denis (1981): *L'usine et son espace*, Paris: Editions de la Villette.

Bowlby, John (1999) [1969]: *Attachment and Loss*, vol. 1, *Attachment*, New York: Basic Books.

Brodwin, Paul (2013): *Everyday Ethics: Voices from the Front Line of Community Psychiatry*, Berkeley: University of California Press.

Buse, Christina, Martin, Daryl & Nettleton, Sarah Joan (2018): "Conceptualising 'Materialities of Care': Making Visible Mundane Material

Culture in Health and Social Care Contexts." In: *Sociology of Health & Illness* 40/2, pp. 243–255.

Callon, Michel (1986): "Some Elements of a Sociology of Translation: Domestication of the Scallops and the Fishermen of St Brieuc Bay." In: Law, John (ed.), *Power, Action and Belief: A New Sociology of Knowledge?*, London: Routledge, pp. 196–223.

Callon, Michel & Law, John (1982): "On Interests and their Transformation: Enrolment and Counter-enrolment." In: *Social Studies of Science* 12/4, pp. 615–625.

Carr, E. Summerson (2010): "Enactments of Expertise." In: *Annual Review of Anthropology* 39/1, pp. 17–32.

Carton, Annabelle, Rousseau, Isabelle, Vandenbussche, Fabrice & Rosenfeld, Boris (2020): "Le voyage de K ou l'expérience d'une trajectoire de soin." In: *Cahiers Critiques de Thérapie Familiale et de Pratiques de Réseaux* 1/64, pp. 129–149.

Classen, Constance (2012): *The Deepest Sense: A Cultural History of Touch*, Urbana: University of Illinois Press.

Cochoy, Fanck (2016 [2011]): *On Curiosity: The Art of Market Seduction*, Manchester: Mattering Press.

Conein, Bernard, Dodier, Nicolas & Thévenot, Laurent (eds.) (1993): *Les objets dans l'action: De la maison au laboratoire*, Paris: Editions de l'Ecole des Hautes Etudes en Sciences Sociales.

Cupers, Kenny (2013): "Introduction." In: Cupers, Kenny (ed.), *Use Matters: An Alternative History of Architecture*, New York: Routledge, pp. 1–12.

d'Hoop, Ariane (2016): "Design through Use for Alternative Psychiatry." In: "Social Poetics. The Architecture of Use and Appropriation", Dehaene, Michiel, Vervloesem, Els, Goethals, Marleen & Yegenoglu, Hüsnü (eds.), special issue, *Oase # 96 Journal for Architecture / Tijdschrift Voor Architectuur*, pp. 37–43.

d'Hoop, Ariane (2020). "Prêter l'oreille en centre de jour." In: *Socio-Anthropologie* 41/1, pp. 103–116.

d'Hoop, Ariane (2021a): "The Moral Life of Doors in an Open Psychiatric Center." In: *Medical Anthropology: Cross Cultural Studies in Health and Illness* 41/1, pp. 67–80.

d'Hoop, Ariane (2021b): "On the Potentialities of Spaces of Care: Openness, Enticement, and Variability in a Psychiatric Center." In: *Science, Technology, & Human Values* 46/3, pp. 577–599.

Debaise, Didier & Stengers, Isabelle (eds.) (2015): *Gestes spéculatifs*, Dijon: Les presses du réel.

Deligny, Fernand, Manenti, Josée & Daniel, Jean-Pierre (1962–1971): *Le moindre geste [The Slightest Gesture]*, Société pour le Lancement des Oeuvres Nouvelles.

Deligny, Fernand, Lin, Jacques & Duran, Gisele (2013): "Cartes et lignes d'erre / Maps and Wander Lines." In: Ogilvie, Bertand & Alvarez de Toledo, Sandra (eds.), *Traces du réseau de Fernand Deligny, 1969–1979*, Paris: Arachnéen.

Demailly, Lise (2011): "La montée des préoccupations gestionnaires en psychiatrie." In: *Sociologie des troubles mentaux*, Paris: La Découverte, pp. 97–103.

Despret, Vinciane (2021 [2019]): *Living as a Bird*, Cambridge & Medford: Polity Press.

Dewey, John (1983 [1916]): *The Middle Works, 1899–1922*, vol. 9, *Democracy and Education*, Carbondale: Southern Illinois University Press.

Dewey, John (2011 [1939]): "Théorie de la valuation." In: *La formation des valeurs*, Paris: Les Empêcheurs de Penser en Rond / La Découverte.

Doucet, Isabelle (2015): "Introduction: The City as a Practice." In: *The practice Turn in Architecture: Brussels after 1968*, Farnham: Ashgate, pp. 1–38.

Doucet, Isabelle, Debaise, Didier & Zitouni, Benedikte (2018): "Narrate, Speculate, Fabulate: Didier Debaise and Benedikte Zitouni in Conversation with Isabelle Doucet." In: Architectural Theory Review 22/1, pp. 9–23.

Doucet, Isabelle & Frichot, Hélène (2018): "Resist, Reclaim, Speculate: Situated Perspectives on Architecture and the City." In: *Architectural Theory Review* 22/1, pp. 1–8.

Driessen, Annelieke (2018): "Sociomaterial Will-Work: Aligning Daily Wanting in Dutch Dementia Care." In: Krause, Franziska & Boldt, Joachim (eds.), *Care in Healthcare: Reflections on Theory and Practice*, London & New York: Palgrave Macmillan, pp. 111–133.

Driessen, Annelieke (2020): "Dementia Matters: User-Building Interactions Shaping Institutional Life in the Netherlands." In: *Medical Anthropology: Cross Cultural Studies in Health and Illness* 39/3, pp. 225–238.

Emerson, Robert M., Fretz, Rachel I. & Shaw, Linda L. (2011 [1995]): *Writing Ethnographic Fieldnotes*, Chicago: University of Chicago Press.

Estroff, Sue (1981): *Making It Crazy: An Ethnography of Psychiatric Clients in an American Community*, Berkeley & Los Angeles: University of California Press.

Evans, Robin (1997[1978]): "Figures, Doors, and Passages." In: *Translations from Drawing to Building and other Essays*, London: Architectural Association, pp. 54–91.

Finkler, Kaja, Hunter, Cynthia & Iedema, Rick (2008): "What Is Going on?: Ethnography in Hospital Spaces." In: *Journal of Contemporary Ethnography* 37/2, pp. 246–250.

Floersch, Jerry (2002): *Meds, Money and Manners: The Case Management of Mental Illness*, New York: Columbia University Press.

Foucault, Michel (1980): *Power/Knowledge: Selected Interviews and Other Writings 1972–1977*, Gordon, Colin (ed.), New York: Pantheon Books.

Foucault, Michel (1995 [1975]): *Discipline and Punish: The Birth of the Prison*, New York: Vintage Books.

Foucault, Michel (2001 [1961]). "Préface de folie et déraison: Histoire de la folie à l'âge classique." In: *Dits et écrits*, vol. 1, 1954–75, Paris: Gallimard, pp. 187–195.

Fussinger, Catherine (2011): "'Therapeutic Community', Psychiatry's Reformers and Antipsychiatrists: Reconsidering Changes in the Field of Psychiatry after World War II." In: *History of Pyschiatry* 22/2, pp.146-163.

Gell, Alfred (1998): *Art and Agency: An Anthropological Theory*, Oxford: Clarendon.

Gibson, James J. (1966): *The Senses Considered as Perceptual Systems*, Boston: Houghton Mifflin.

Gibson, James J. (1986 [1979]): *The Ecological Approach to Visual Perception*, New York & London: Taylor & Francis.

Gieryn, Thomas F. (2000): "A Space for Place in Sociology." In: *Annual Review of Sociology* 26, pp. 463–496.

Gieryn, Thomas F. (2002): "What Buildings Do." In: *Theory and Society: Renewal and Critique of Social Theory* 31, pp. 35–74.

Gijswijt-Hofstra, Marijke, Oosterhuis, Harry, Vijselaar, Joost & Freeman, Hugh (eds.) (2005): *Psychiatric Cultures Compared: Psychiatry and Mental Health Care in the Twentieth Century*, Amsterdam: Amsterdam University Press.

Goffman, Ervin (1961): *Asylums: Essays on the Social Situation of Mental Patients and Other Inmates*, New York: Anchor Books.

Goffman, Ervin (1963): *Behavior in Public Places: Notes on the Social Organization of Gatherings*, New York: The Free Press.

Goffman, Ervin (1971): *Relations in Public: Microstudies of the Public Order*, New York: Basic Books.

Gomart, Emilie & Hennion, Antoine (1999): "A Sociology of Attachment: Music, Amateurs, Drug Users." In: Law, John & Hassard, John (eds.), *Actor Network Theory and After*, Oxford & Malden: Blackwell, pp. 220–247.

Guattari, Félix (ed.) (1967): "*Programmation architecture et psychiatrie.*" Numéro spécial, *Revue Recherches* 6/juin 1967.

Guedez, Annie (2004): "La 'belle maison' dans la Grande Lande." In: Nahoum-Grappe, Véronique & Vincent, Odile (eds.), *Le goût des belles choses. Ethnologie de la relation esthétique*, Paris: Maison des Sciences de l'Homme, pp. 49–65.

Guggenheim, Michael (2013): "Unifying and Decomposing Building Types: How to Analyze the Change of Use of Sacred Buildings." In: *Qualitative Sociology* 36, pp. 445–464.

Hall, Edward T. (1966): *The Hidden Dimension*, New-York: Anchor Books.

Hamlett, Jane (2015): *At Home in the Institution: Material Life in Asylums, Lodging Houses and Schools in Victorian and Edwardian England*, London: Palgrave Macmillan.

Haraway, Donna (1988) "Situated Knowledge: The Science Question in Feminism and the Privilege of Partial Perspective." In: *Feminist Studies* 14/3, pp. 575–599.

Haraway, Donna (2007): *When Species Meet*, Minneapolis: University of Minnesota Press.

Helmreich, Stefan (2014): "Waves. An Anthropology of Scientific Things: Transcript of the Lewis Henry Morgan Lecture Given on October 22, 2014." In: *HAU: Journal of Ethnographic Theory* 4/3, pp. 265–289.

Hendriks, Ruud (2012): "Tackling Indifference: Clowning, Dementia, and the Articulation of a Sensitive Body." In: *Medical Anthropology: Cross Cultural Studies in Health and Illness* 31/6, pp. 459–476.

Hennion, Antoine (1988): "'Qu'entends-tu?': Ethnographie d'une classe de solfège." In: *Comment la musique vient aux enfants. Une anthropologie de l'enseignement musical*, Paris: Anthropos, pp. 5–32.

Hennion, Antoine (2004): "Une sociologie des attachements. D'une sociologie de la culture à une pragmatique de l'amateur." In: *Sociétés* 85/3, pp. 9–24.

Hennion, Antoine (2005): "Pragmatics of Taste." In: Jacobs, Mark D. & Hanrahan, Nancy W. (eds.), *The Blackwell Companion to the Sociology of Culture*, Oxford: Blackwell, pp. 131–144.

Hennion, Antoine (2007): "Those Things that Hold us Together: Taste and Sociology." In: *Cultural Sociology* 1/1, pp. 97–114.

Hennion, Antoine (2009): "Réflexivités: L'activité de l'amateur." In: *Réseaux, Communication, Technologie et Société* 1/153, pp. 55–78.

Hennion, Antoine (2015[1993]): *The Passion for Music: A Sociology of Mediation*, Surrery: Ashgate.

Hennion, Antoine (2017): "Attachments, You Say? … How a Concept Collectively Emerges in One Research Group." In: *Journal of Cultural Economy* 10/1, pp. 112–121.

Hennion, Antoine, Gomart, Emilie & Maisonneuve, Sophie (2000): *Figures de l'amateur. Formes, objets, pratiques de l'amour de la musique aujourd'hui*, Paris: La Documentation Française.

Hennion, Antoine & Teil, Geneviève (2004): "Le goût du vin. Pour une sociologie de l'attention." In: Nahoum-Grappe, Véronique & Vincent, Odile (eds.), *Le goût des belles choses. Ethnologie de la relation esthétique*, Paris: Maison des Sciences de l'Homme, pp. 111–126.

Hirschauer, Stefan (2005): "On Doing Being a Stranger: The Practical Constitution of Civil Inattention." In: *Journal for the Theory of Social Behavior* 35/1, pp. 41–67.

Hirschauer, Stefan (2006): "Puttings Things into Words. Ethnographic Description and the Silence of the Social." In: *Human Studies: A Journal for Philosophy and the Social Sciences* 29, pp. 413–441.

Houdart, Sophie (2009): *Kuma Kengo: An Unconventional Monograph*, Paris: Donner Lieu.

Ingold, Tim (2011 [1995]): "Building, Dwelling, Living: How Animals and People Make Themselves at Home in the World." In: *The Perception of the Environment: Essays on Livelihood, Dwelling and Skill*, London: Routledge, pp. 172–188.

Ingold, Tim & Vergunst, Jo Lee (eds.) (2008): *Ways of Walking: Ethnography and Practice on Foot*, Aldershot: Ashgate.

Jenkins, Janis H. & Csordas, Thomas (2020): *Troubled in the Land of Enchantment: Adolescent Experience of Psychiatric Treatment*, Oakland: University of California Press.

Jones, Maxwell (1953): *The Therapeutic Community: A New Treatment Method in Psychiatry*, New York: Basic Books.

Knowles, Caroline (2000): *Bedlam on the Streets*, London: Routledge.

Koolhaas, Rem, Petermann, Stephan, Trüby, Stephan, & di Robilant, Manfredo (2014): *Elements*, Venezia: Marsilio.

Kovess-Masféty, Viviane, Severo, Donato, Causse, David & Pascal, Jean-Charles (2004): *Architecture et psychiatrie*, Paris: Le Moniteur.

Laget, Pierre-Louis (2008): "Les missions à l'étranger. Des moyens de réinventer l'architecture hospitalière (du XVIIIe au XXe siècle)." In: Dinet-Lecomte, Marie-Claude (ed.), *Les hôpitaux, enjeux de pouvoir: France du nord et Belgique, IVe-XXe siècle*, Hors série Histoire, *Revue du Nord* 22, pp. 267–288.

Laget, Pierre-Louis, Laroche, Claude & Duhau, Isabelle (2016 [2012]): *L'hôpital en France. Du Moyen Âge à nos jours, Histoire et architecture*, Lyon: Lieux Dits.

Lapoujade, David (2021 [2017]): *The Lesser Existences: Etienne Souriau, an Aesthetics for the Virtual*, Minneapolis & London: University of Minnesota Press.

Latour, Bruno (1991): *Nous n'avons jamais été modernes. Essai d'anthropologie symétrique*, Paris: La Découverte.

Latour, Bruno (1996 [1994]): "On Interobjectivity." In: *Mind, Culture, and Activity* 3/4, pp. 228–245.

Latour, Bruno (1999): "Factures/Fractures: From the Concept of Network to the Concept of Attachment." In: *Res* 36/36, pp. 20–31.

Latour, Bruno (2004): "Why Has Critique Run out of Steam? From Matters of Fact to Matters of Concern." In: *Critical Inquiry* 30/2, pp. 225–248.

Latour, Bruno (2008 [1992]): "Where Are the Missing Masses? The Sociology of a Few Mundane Artefacts." In: Johnson, Deborah J. & Wetmore, Jameson M. (eds.), *Technology and Society, Building Our Sociotechnical Future*, Cambridge: MIT Press, pp. 151–180.

Law, John (2009): "Actor Network Theory and Material Semiotics." In: Turner, Bryan S. (ed.), *The New Blackwell Companion to Social Theory*, Oxford: Blackwell, pp. 142–158.

Law, John & Moser, Ingunn (1999): "Good Passages, Bad Passages" In: Law, John & Hassard, John (eds.), *Actor Network Theory and After*, Oxford & Malden Blackwell, pp. 196–219.

Laws, Jennifer (2009): "Reworking Therapeutic Landscapes: The Spatiality of an 'Alternative' Self-help Group." In: *Social Science & Medicine* 69, pp. 1827–1833.

Lie, Kveim Anne & Green, Jeremy (2021): "Introduction to Special Issue: Psychiatry as Social Medicine." In: *Culture, Medicine, and Psychiatry: An International Journal of Cross-Cultural Health Research* 45, pp. 333–342.

Livingstone, Julie (2012): *Improvising Medicine: An African Oncology Ward in an Emerging Cancer Epidemic*, Durham & London: Duke University Press.

Long, Debbi, Hunter, Cynthia & van der Geest, Sjaak (2008): "When the Field is a Ward or a Clinic: Hospital Ethnography." In: *Anthropology & Medicine* 15/2, pp. 71–78.

Luckhurst, Roger (2019): *Corridors, Passages of Modernity*, London: Reaktion Books.

Lurhmann, Tanya M. (2000): *Of Two Minds: An Anthropologist Looks at American Psychiatry*, New York: Vintage.

Majerus, Benoît (2013): *Parmi les fous. Une histoire sociale de la psychiatrie au XXe siècle*, Rennes: Presses Universitaires de Rennes.

Markus, Thomas. A. (1993): *Buildings and Power: Freedom and Control in the Origin of Modern Building Types*, London: Routledge.

Martin, Daryl (2016): "Curating Space, Choreographing Care: The Efficacy of the Everyday." In Bates, Charlotte, Imrie, Rob & Kullman, Kim (eds.), *Care and Design: Bodies, Buildings, Cities*, Oxford: Wiley-Blackwell, pp. 37–55.

Martin, Daryl, Nettleton, Sarah, Buse, Christina, Prior, Lindsay & Twigg, Julia (2015): "Architecture and Health Care: A Place for Sociology." In: *Sociology of Health & Illness* 37/7, pp. 1007–1022.

Martin, Emily (2007): *Bipolar Expeditions: Mania and Depression in American Culture*, Princeton: Princeton University Press.

M'charek, Amade (2014): "Race, Time and Folded Objects: The HeLa Error" In: Theory, Culture & Society 31/6, pp. 29–56.

Mens, Noor & Wagenaar, Cor (2010): *Health Care Architecture in the Netherlands*, Rotterdam: NAI.

Michael, Robert B., Garry, Marianne & Kirsch, Irving (2012): "Suggestion, Cognition, and Behavior." In: *Current Directions in Psychological Science* 21/3, pp. 151–156.

Miguel, Marlon (2014): "Somewhere in the Cévennes circa 1970. Experienceing Space and Spacing Experience in Fernand Deligny's Network." In Berning, Nora, Schulte, Philipp & Schwanecke, Christine (eds.), *Experiencing Space – Spacing Experience: Concepts, Practices and Materialities*, Trier: Wissenschaftlicher, pp. 111–127.

Mol, Annemarie (2002): *The Body Multiple: Ontology in Medical Practice*, Durham: Duke University Press.

Mol, Annemarie (2008): *The Logic of Care: Health and the Problem of Patient Choice*, London & New York: Routledge.

Mol, Annemarie (2010): "Care and its Values: Good Food in the Nursing Home" In: Mol, Annemarie, Moser, Ingunn & Pols, Jeannette (eds.): *Care in Practice: On Tinkering in Clinics, Homes and Farms*, Bielefeld: transcript, pp. 215–234.

Mol, Annemarie, Moser, Ingunn & Pols, Jeannette (2010) (eds.): *Care in Practice: On Tinkering in Clinics, Homes and Farms*, Bielefeld: transcript.

Murard, Lion & Fourquet, François (eds.) (1975): "Histoire de la psychiatrie de secteur ou le secteur impossible." Numéro spécial, *Revue Recherches* 17/mars 1975.

Myers, Neely L. (2015): *Recovery's Edge: An Ethnography of Mental Health Care and Moral Agency*, Nashville: Vanderbilt University Press.

Nathan, Tobie (1994): *L'influence qui guérit*, Paris: Odile Jacob.

Nathan, Tobie (2001): *Nous ne sommes pas seuls au monde: Les enjeux de l'ethnopsychiatrie*, Paris: Seuil.

Nord, Catharina & Högström, Ebba (eds.) (2017): *Caring Architecture: Institutions and Relational Practices*, Newcastle, UK: Cambridge Scholars Press.

Norman, Donald A. (1998 [1988]): *The Design of Everyday Things*, Cambridge, MA: MIT Press.

Oxford English Dictionary online, s.v. "Familiarity", accessed December 04, 2016, https://www.oed.com.

Pasveer, Bernike, Synnes, Oddgeir & Moser, Ingunn (eds.) (2019): *Ways of Home Making in Care for Later Life*, Singapore: Springer Nature.

Philibert, Nicolas (1997): *La moindre des choses*. [*Every Little Thing*], La Sept Cinéma; Les Films d'Ici.

Pols, Jeannette (2005): "Enacting Appreciations: Beyond the Patient Perspective." In: *Health Care Analysis* 13/3, pp. 203–221.

Pols, Jeannette (2010): "Breathtaking Practicalities: A Politics of Embodied Patient Positions." In: *Scandinavian Journal of Disability Research* 13/3, pp. 1–18.

Pols, Jeannette (2012): *Care at a Distance: On the Closeness of Technology*, Amsterdam: Amsterdam University Press.

Pols, Jeannette (2015): "Towards an Empirical Ethics in Care: Relations with Technologies in Health Care." In: *Medicine, Health Care and Philosophy* 18/1, pp. 81–90.

Pols, Jeannette (unpublished manuscript): *The Good Life: An Empirical Contribution to the Philosophy of Care*.

Prior, Lindsay (1988): "The Architecture of the Hospital: A Study of Spatial Organization and Medical Knowledge." In: *The British Journal of Sociology* 39/1, pp. 86–113.

Quétel, Claude (2010): *Images de la folie*, Paris: Gallimard.

Rafanell i Orra, Josep (2011): *En finir avec le capitalisme thérapeutique. Soin, politique et communauté*, Paris: les Empêcheurs de penser en rond / La Découverte.

Rhodes, Lorna (1991): *Emptying Beds: The Work of an Emergency Psychiatric Unit*, Berkeley: University of California Press.

Richelle, Marc (2007 [1991]): "Décharge" In: Doron, Roland & Parot, Françoise (eds.), *Dictionnaire de psychologie*, Paris: Presses Universitaires de France, p. 182.

Rogers, Carl R. (2020 [1967]): *On Becoming a Person: A Therapist's View of Psychotherapy*, London: Constable & Robinson.

Rose, Deborah Bird (2004): *Reports from a Wild Country: Ethics for Decolonisation*, Sydney: University of New South Wales Press.

Rosenberg, Daniel & Grafton, Anthony (2010): *Cartographies of Time: A History of the Timeline*, New York: Princeton Architectural Press.

Rotor (Gielen, Maarten, Boniver, Tristan, Devlieger, Lionel, Ghyoot, Michael, Lasserre, Benjamin, Tamm, Mélanie), d'Hoop, Ariane & Zitouni, Benedikte (2010): *Usus/Usures: Etats des lieux / How Things Stand*, Bruxelles: Communauté française de Belgique.

Rozier, Emmanuelle (2014): *La clinique de La Borde ou les relations qui soignent: Outils philosophiques pour comprendre le collectif*, Toulouse: Erès.

Sacks, Oliver (2012 [1995]): *An Anthropologist on Mars*, London: Picador.

Segaud, Marion, Brun, Jacques & Driant, Jean-Claude (2002): *Dictionnaire de l'habitat et du logement*, s.v. "appropriation", Paris: Armand Colin, pp. 27–30.

Sennett, Richard (1976): *Flesh and Stone: The Body and the City in Western Culture*, New York: W. W. Norton & Company

Sennett, Richard (2008): *The Craftsman*, New Haven & London: Yale University Press.

Serres, Michel & Latour, Bruno (1995): *Conversations on Science, Culture and Time*, Ann Arbor: University of Michigan Press.

Smith, Yvonne & Spitzmueller, Matthew C. (2016): "Worker Perspectives on Contemporary Milieu Therapy: A Cross-site Ethnographic Study." In: *Social Worker Research* 40/2, pp. 105–116.

Spandler, Helen (2015): *Asylum to Action: Paddington Day Hospital, Therapeutic Communities and Beyond*, London: Jessica Kingsley.

Stengers, Isabelle (2006): *La volonté de faire sciences. A propos de la psychanalyse*, Paris Les Empêcheurs de penser en Rond / La Découverte.

Street, Alice (2012): *Biomedicine in an Unstable Place: Infrastructure and Personhood in a Papua New Guinean Hospital*, Durham & London: Duke University Press.

Street, Alice & Coleman, Simon (2012): "Introduction: Real and Imagined Spaces." In: *Space and Culture* 15/1, pp. 4–17.

Thévenot, Laurent (1994): "Régime de familiarité. Des choses en personne." In: *Genèses. Sciences sociales et histoire* 17/1, pp. 72–101.

Thévenot, Laurent (1997): "Le savoir au travail. Attribution et distribution des compétences selon les régimes pragmatiques." In: Reynaud, Bénédicte (ed.), *Les limites de la rationalité. Tome 2. Les figures du collectif*, Paris: La Découverte, pp. 299–321.

Thévenot, Laurent (2001): "Pragmatic Regimes Governing the Engagement with the World." In: Schatzki, Theodore R., Knorr Cetina, Karin & von Savigny, Eike, *The Practice Turn in Contemporary Theory*, London: Routledge, pp. 77–82.

Topp, Leslie E., Moran, James E. & Andrews, Jonathan (eds.) (2007): *Madness, Architecture and the Built Environment: Psychiatric Spaces in Historical Context*, New York & London: Routledge.

Troisoeufs, Aurélien (2009): "La personne intermédiaire. Hôpital psychiatrique et groupe d'entraide mutuelle." In: *Terrain* 52, pp. 96–111.

Tsing, Anna L. (2015): *The Mushroom at the End of the World: On the Possibility of Life in Capitalist Ruins*, Princeton: Princeton University Press.

Twigg, Julia (1999): "The spatial Ordering of Care: Public and Private in Bathing Support at Home." In: *Sociology of Health & Illness* 2/4, pp. 381–400.

Van Hout, Annemarie, Pols, Jeannette & Willems, Dick (2015): "Shining Trinkets and Unkempt Gardens: On the Materiality of Care." In: *Sociology of Health & Illness* 37/8, pp. 1206–1217.

Velpry, Livia (2008): *Le quotidien de la psychiatrie. Sociologie de la maladie mentale*, Paris: Armand Colin.

Vermeylen, Jean & Schouters-Decroly, Lucette (2001): *Hors les murs! Naissance de la psychiatrie extrahospitalière. L'Équipe: histoire et philosophie,* Bruxelles: Groupe secteur recherche.

Veron, Eliseo & Levasseur, Martine (1989): *Ethnographie de l'exposition. L'espace, le corps, le sens,* Paris: BPI du Centre Pompidou.

Vogel, Else & Mol, Annemarie (2014): "Enjoy your Food: On Losing Weight and Taking Pleasure" In: *Sociology of Health & Illness* 36/2, pp. 305–317.

Vugts, Anastasia, van den Hoven, Mariëtte, de Vet, Emely & Verweij, Marcel (2020): "How Autonomy Is Understood in Discussions on the Ethics of Nudging" In: *Behavioural Public Policy* 4/1, pp. 108–123.

Walker, Carole, Nicaise, Pablo & Thunus, Sophie (2019): *Parcours. Bruxelles: Evaluation qualitative du système de la santé mentale et des parcours des usagers dans le cadre de la réforme Psy 107 en Région de Bruxelles-Capitale,* Bruxelles: Observatoire de la santé et du social.

Whyte, William H. (1980): *The Social Life of Small Urban Spaces,* New York: Project for Public Spaces Inc.

Wilkinson, Eleanor (2014): "Single People's Geographies of Home: Intimacy and Friendship beyond 'the Family'." In: *Environment and Planning A: Economy and Space* 46/10, pp. 2452–2468.

Winance, Myriam (2019): "'Don't Touch/Push Me!' From Disruption to Intimacy in Relations with One's Wheelchair: An Analysis of Relational Modalities between Persons and Objects." In: *The Sociological Review Monographs* 67/2, pp. 428–443.

Winkin, Yves (2016 [1988]): "Portrait du sociologue en jeune homme." In *Erving Goffman: Les moments et leurs hommes,* Paris: Seuil, pp. 11–114.

Winnicott, Donald W. (1965): *The Maturational Processes and the Facilitating Environment: Studies in the Theory of Emotional Development,* New York: International Universities Press.

Wolch, Jennifer & Philo, Chris (2000): "From Distributions of Deviance to Definitions of Difference: Past and Future Mental Health Geographies." In: *Health & Place* 6/3, pp. 137–157.

Woolf, Virginia (2000 [1931]): *The Waves,* Hertfordshire: Wordsworth.

Yaneva, Albena (2009a): *The Making of a Building: A Pragmatist Approach to Architecture,* Oxford: Peter Lang.

Yaneva, Albena (2009b): "Border Crossings. Making the Social Hold: Towards an Actor-Network Theory of Design." In: *Design and Culture* 1/3, pp. 273–288.

Yanni, Carla (2006): "Beyond the Hospital: The Clubhouse Model for Psychiatric Patients." In: Wagenaar, Cor (ed.), *The Architecture of Hospitals*, Rotterdam: NAI, pp. 432–442.

Yanni, Carla (2007): *The Architecture of Madness: Insane Asylums in the United States*, Minneapolis: University of Minnesota Press.

Zaccaï-Reyners, Nathalie (2015): "Quand les relations quotidiennes sont à ré-imaginer: éclairages à partir du jeu." In Mermet, Laurent & Zaccaï-Reyners, Nathalie (eds.), *Au prisme du jeu. Concepts, pratiques, perspectives*, Paris: Hermann, pp. 245–267.

Social Sciences

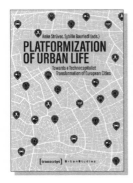

Anke Strüver, Sybille Bauriedl (eds.)
Platformization of Urban Life
Towards a Technocapitalist Transformation
of European Cities

September 2022, 304 p., pb.
29,50 € (DE), 978-3-8376-5964-1
E-Book: available as free open access publication
PDF: ISBN 978-3-8394-5964-5

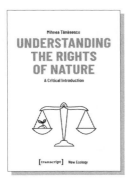

Mihnea Tanasescu
Understanding the Rights of Nature
A Critical Introduction

February 2022, 168 p., pb.
40,00 € (DE), 978-3-8376-5431-8
E-Book: available as free open access publication
PDF: ISBN 978-3-8394-5431-2

Oliver Krüger
Virtual Immortality –
God, Evolution, and the Singularity
in Post- and Transhumanism

2021, 356 p., pb., ill.
35,00 € (DE), 978-3-8376-5059-4
E-Book:
PDF: 34,99 € (DE), ISBN 978-3-8394-5059-8

All print, e-book and open access versions of the titles in our list
are available in our online shop www.transcript-publishing.com

Social Sciences

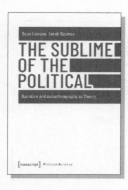

Dean Caivano, Sarah Naumes
The Sublime of the Political
Narrative and Autoethnography as Theory

2021, 162 p., hardcover
100,00 € (DE), 978-3-8376-4772-3
E-Book:
PDF: 99,99 € (DE), ISBN 978-3-8394-4772-7

Friederike Landau, Lucas Pohl, Nikolai Roskamm (eds.)
[Un]Grounding
Post-Foundational Geographies

2021, 348 p., pb., col. ill.
50,00 € (DE), 978-3-8376-5073-0
E-Book:
PDF: 49,99 € (DE), ISBN 978-3-8394-5073-4

Andreas de Bruin
Mindfulness and Meditation at University
10 Years of the Munich Model

2021, 216 p., pb.
25,00 € (DE), 978-3-8376-5696-1
E-Book: available as free open access publication
PDF: ISBN 978-3-8394-5696-5